UNIT

AQA A2 4

Biology

Populations and Environment

Steve Potter

Philip Allan Updates, an imprint of Hodder Education, an Hachette UK company, Market Place, Deddington, Oxfordshire OX15 0SE

Orders

Bookpoint Ltd, 130 Milton Park, Abingdon, Oxfordshire OX14 4SB
tel: 01235 827827
fax: 01235 400401
e-mail: education@bookpoint.co.uk

Lines are open 9.00 a.m.–5.00 p.m., Monday to Saturday, with a 24-hour message answering service. You can also order through the Philip Allan Updates website: www.philipallan.co.uk

ISBN 978-0-340-94952-8

First printed 2009
Impression number 5 4 3
Year 2014 2013 2012 2011

This guide has been written specifically to support students preparing for the AQA A2 Biology Unit 4 examination. The content has been neither approved nor endorsed by AQA and remains the sole responsibility of the author.

Typeset by DC Graphic Design, Swanley Village, Kent
Printed by MPG Books, Bodmin

Hachette UK's policy is to use papers that are natural, renewable and recyclable products and made from wood grown in sustainable forests. The logging and manufacturing processes are expected to conform to the environmental regulations of the country of origin.

Contents

Introduction

■ ■ ■

Content Guidance

■ ■ ■

Questions and Answers

Introduction

About this guide

This guide is written to help you to prepare for the Unit 4 examination of the new AQA Biology specification. The Unit 4 examination examines the content of **Unit 4: Populations and Environment**, and forms part of the A2 assessment.

This **Introduction** provides guidance on revision, together with advice on approaching the unit examination.

The **Content Guidance** section gives a point-by-point description of all the facts you need to know and concepts you need to understand for Unit 4. In each topic, the concepts are presented first. It is a good idea to get your mind around these key ideas before you try to learn all the associated facts.

The **Question and Answer** section shows you the sorts of question you can expect in the unit examination. It would be impossible to give examples of every kind of question in one book, but these should give you a flavour of what to expect. Each question has been attempted by two candidates, Candidate A and Candidate B. Their answers, along with the examiner's comments, should help you to see what you need to do to score a good mark — and how you can easily *not* score a mark even though you may understand the biology.

What can I assume about the guide?

You can assume that:
- the basic facts you need to know and understand are stated explicitly
- the major concepts you need to understand are explained clearly
- the questions at the end of the guide are similar in style to those that will appear in the end-of-unit examination
- the answers supplied are the answers of A2 students
- the standard of the marking is broadly equivalent to the standard that will be applied to your answers

What can I *not* assume about the guide?

You *must not* assume that:
- the diagrams used will be the same as those used in the end-of-unit examination (they may be more or less detailed, seen from a different angle etc.)
- the way in which the concepts are explained is the *only* way in which they can be presented in an examination (concepts are often presented in an unfamiliar situation)
- the range of question types presented is exhaustive (examiners are always thinking of new ways to test a topic)

How Science Works

This is a new component in the biology specifications of all examination boards. The aim is to help you to understand the *process* of scientific work. You will not find any specific section devoted to 'How Science Works' (HSW) in this guide, but the main aspects of HSW are described below:

- Scientists use pre-existing knowledge and understanding/theories/models to suggest explanations for phenomena.
- They design, carry out, analyse and evaluate scientific investigations to test new explanations.
- They share their findings with other scientists so that they may (or not) be validated.

As a consequence of the work of scientists, there may be implications for society as a whole. You are expected to appreciate and make informed (not emotional) comment on such aspects as:

- the ethical implications of the way in which research is carried out
- the way in which society uses science to help in decision making

Some of the questions in the Question and Answer section address HSW.

So how should I use this guide?

The guide lends itself to a number of uses throughout your course — it is not *just* a revision aid. You can use it:

- to check that your notes cover the material required by the specification
- to identify strengths and weaknesses
- as a reference for homework and internal tests
- during your revision to prepare 'bite-sized' chunks of related material, rather than being faced with a file full of notes

The Question and Answer section can be used to:

- identify the terms used by examiners in questions and what they expect of you
- familiarise yourself with the style of questions you can expect
- identify the ways in which marks are lost as well as how they are gained

Preparing for the Unit 4 examination

Preparation for examinations is a personal thing. Different people prepare, equally successfully, in different ways. The key is being honest about what actually *works* for *you*.

Whatever your style, you must have a plan. Sitting down the night before the examination with a file full of notes and a textbook does not constitute a revision plan — it is just desperation — and you must not expect a great deal from it. Whatever your personal style, there are a number of things you *must* do and a number of other things you *could* do.

Things you *must* do

- Leave yourself enough time to cover all the material.
- Make sure that you actually *have* all the material to hand (use this book as a basis).
- Identify weaknesses early in your preparation so that you have time to do something about them.
- Familiarise yourself with the terminology used in examination questions (see below).

Things you *could* do to help you learn

Psychologists have shown that you learn facts and ideas better if you are *active* in your learning. Just reading your notes over and over again is not a good way of revising. Instead, you could:

- write a summary of your notes that includes all the key points
- write key points on postcards (carry them round with you for quick revision during a coffee break)
- discuss a topic with a friend who is studying the same course
- try to explain a topic to someone not on the course
- practise answering examination questions on the topic

All these techniques make you *think* about the material. The more you *process* the information as you revise, the more effective your revision will be.

Approaching the Unit 4 examination

Terms used in examination questions

You will be asked precise questions in the examination, so you can save a lot of valuable time and ensure that you score as many marks as possible by knowing what is expected. Terms most commonly used are explained below.

- **Describe** — this means exactly what it says — 'tell me about...' — and you should not need to explain why.
- **Explain** — give biological reasons for *why* or *how* something is happening.
- **Complete** — finish off a diagram, graph, flow chart or table.
- **Draw/plot** — construct some type of graph. For this, make sure that:
  - you choose a scale that makes good use of the graph paper (if a scale is not given) and does not leave all the plots tucked away in one corner
  - plot an appropriate type of graph — if both variables are continuous variables, then a line graph is usually the most appropriate; if one is a discrete variable, then a bar chart is appropriate
  - plot carefully using a sharp pencil and draw lines accurately

- **From the...** — use only information in the diagram/graph/photograph or other forms of data.
- **Name** — give the name of a structure/molecule/organism etc.
- **Suggest** — i.e. 'give a plausible biological explanation for'; this term is often used when testing understanding of concepts in an unfamiliar situation.
- **Compare** — give similarities *and* differences between...
- **Calculate** — add, subtract, multiply, divide (do some kind of sum) and show how you got your answer — *always* show your working.

The examination

When you finally open the exam paper, it can be a stressful moment. You may not recognise the diagram or graph used in question 1. It can be demoralising to attempt a question at the start of an examination if you are not feeling confident about it. The following advice should help you achieve a good result.

- Do *not* begin to write as soon as you open the paper.
- Do *not* necessarily answer question 1 first, just because it is printed first (the examiner did not sequence the questions with your particular favourites in mind).
- Scan *all* the questions before you begin to answer any.
- Identify those questions about which you feel most confident.
- Answer *first* those questions about which you feel most confident, regardless of the order in the paper.
- *Read the question carefully* — if you are asked to explain, then explain, don't just describe.
- Take notice of the mark allocation. Don't supply the examiner with all your knowledge of osmosis if there is only 1 mark allocated (similarly, you have to come up with four ideas if 4 marks are allocated).
- Try to stick to the point in your answer (it is easy to stray into related areas that will not score marks and that will use up valuable time).
- Take particular care with:
  - drawings — you will not be asked to produce complex diagrams, but those you do produce must resemble the subject
  - labelling — label lines *must touch* the part you are required to identify; if they stop short or pass through the part, you will lose marks
  - graphs — draw *small* points if you are asked to plot a graph and join the plots with ruled lines or, if specifically asked for, a line or smooth curve of best fit through all the plots
- Try to answer *all* the questions.

Content
Guidance

This section is a guide to the content of **Unit 4: Populations and Environment**. The main areas of this module are:

- populations and ecosystems
- photosynthesis
- respiration
- the transfer of energy through ecosystems
- the cycling of nutrients through ecosystems
- patterns of inheritance
- selection and speciation

Key facts you must know and understand

These are exactly what you might think: a summary of all the basic knowledge that you must be able to recall and show that you understand. The knowledge has been broken down into a number of small facts that you must learn. This means that the list of 'Key facts' for some topics is quite long. However, this approach makes quite clear *everything* you need to know about the topic.

Key concepts you must understand

These are a little different. Whereas you can learn facts, these are ideas or concepts that often form the basis of models that we use to explain aspects of biology. You can know the actual words that describe a concept like osmosis, or the resolving power of a microscope, but you will not be able to use this information unless you really understand what is going on. Once you genuinely understand a concept, you will probably not have to learn it again.

What the examiners could ask you to do

This part tries to give you an insight into the minds of the examiners who will set and mark your examination papers. They may ask you to recall any of the basic knowledge or explain any of the key concepts; but they may well do more than that. Examiners think up questions where the concepts you understand are in a different setting or context from the one(s) you are familiar with. This could include the evaluation of data under the 'How Science Works' requirement, set in the context of this particular topic.

Bear in mind that examiners will often set individual questions that involve knowledge and understanding of more than one section. The sample questions in the Question and Answer section of this book will help you to practise drawing together material from different areas of the specification.

Populations and the factors that affect them
Populations and ecosystems

Key concepts you must understand

Ecosystem

An ecosystem is a self-supporting system of organisms interacting with each other and with their physical environment. Interactions between organisms include:

- competition for resources:
  - food, mates, territory (animals)
  - light, carbon dioxide, water, mineral ions (plants)
- feeding relationships — plants, herbivores, carnivores and decomposers all pass the same recycled nutrients through food webs

Ecosystems vary greatly in size. A garden pond could be considered an ecosystem, as could a tropical rainforest.

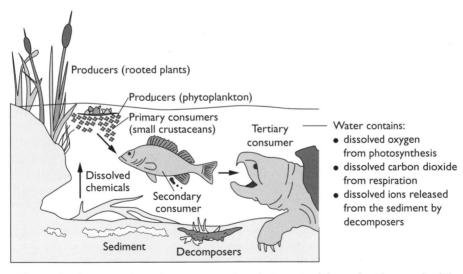

Figure 1 The organisms in an ecosystem interact with each other and with their physical environments

Community

A community is the sum of *all* the organisms in an ecosystem. This includes the producers, the consumers and the decomposers.

Population

All the individuals of one particular species found in an ecosystem at any given time.

Environment

The environment of an organism is the sum of all the conditions or factors in the ecosystem outside the organism. It is made up of a **biotic** (living) component and an **abiotic** (non-living) component. The biotic component is the sum of those factors that are caused by the activities of other organisms. However, the term environment is usually taken to mean the physical environment — the abiotic factors. Both biotic and abiotic factors can influence the size of populations.

Habitat

A habitat is the place within an ecosystem where a particular population is found. In a pond, tadpoles tend to inhabit shallow warm water (if the food supply is adequate).

Niche

A niche is not just a place where a species is found (that is the habitat). A niche includes a description of how the species functions in that place. Several species of bird can inhabit the same tree, even the same areas of the same tree. However, if

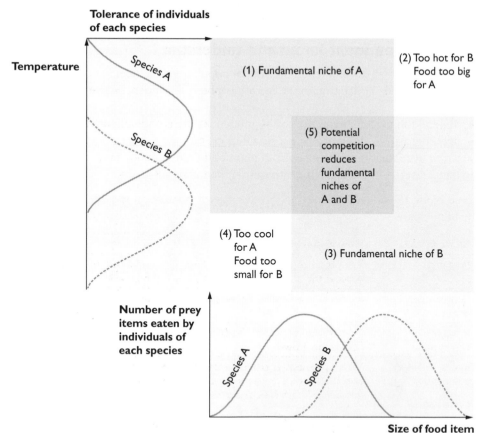

When the two environmental factors (one biotic and one abiotic) are combined, there is only a small area of overlap between the two species. This is represented by region 5 in the diagram.

Figure 2 *Different organisms have different niches*

they feed at different times of the day or on different sized insects or use different materials for their nests, they are occupying different niches and are not in direct competition with each other for the available resources.

Factors affecting population size

Key concepts you must understand

Population size is dependent on the availability of resources. If resources are essentially unlimited, then a population will continue growing. Both biotic and abiotic factors can restrict population growth.

One key biotic factor is competition for resources. There are two types of competition:

- **interspecific competition** — competition for resources between members of *different* species
- **intraspecific competition** — competition between members of the *same* species

Key facts you must know and understand

Abiotic factors that can influence the size of populations include:

- carbon dioxide concentration in the atmosphere — influences plant populations only
- mineral ion availability in the soil — influences plant populations only
- light intensity — influences plant populations only
- water availability — influences both plant and animal populations
- temperature — influences both plant and animal populations

Some biotic factors and their effect on the size of population growth are shown in the table below.

Biotic factor	How it affects population size
Predation	The presence of a predator (or herbivore in the case of plants) reduces the numbers in the prey (or plant) population.
Disease-causing organisms	If disease is widespread, then population growth is slowed.
Intraspecific competition	Competition between members of the same species reduces population growth.
Interspecific competition	When two species compete for the same resource, either one of the two species outcompetes the other or the two species coexist, but numbers of both species are reduced.

The predator–prey relationship

One of the best-known examples of the relationship between a predator and its prey is that between the snowshoe hare and the lynx.

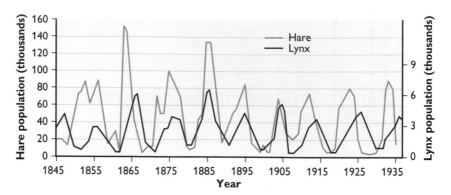

Figure 3 Changes in the population size of showshoe hare and lynx from 1845 to 1935

The population sizes of predator and prey are interdependent:
- An increase in the population of the prey means more food for the predator.
- The predator population increases.
- The increased numbers of predators kill more prey, so the prey population decreases.
- There is now less food for the predator, so the predator population decreases.
- The reduced numbers of predators kill less prey, so the prey numbers increase.

The change in the numbers of the predator population always lags behind that of the prey population. This is because the predator is dependent on the prey for food. Notice that the number of predators is always lower than the number of prey. This is because of the loss of energy along a food chain.

Interspecific competition

When different species of *Paramecium* are grown in isolation, each population reaches a natural limit (see Figure 4).

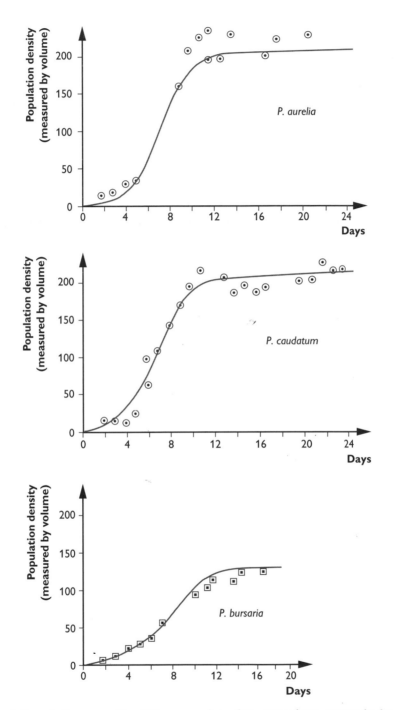

Figure 4 Population growth of three species of Paramecium grown in isolation

When *Paramecium caudatum* and *Paramecium aurelia* are grown together, *Paramecium aurelia* outcompetes *Paramecium caudatum*, which becomes locally extinct.

When *Paramecium caudatum* and *Paramecium bursaria* are grown together, the species coexist, but with reduced population levels.

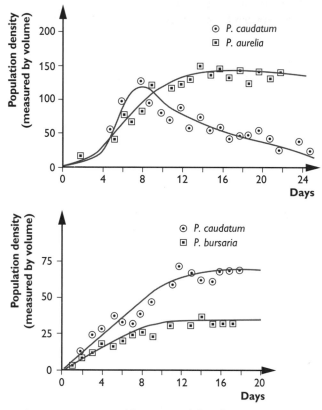

Figure 5 Interspecific competition in Paramecium

Investigating populations

Key concepts you must understand

It is usually impossible to count all the organisms in a population, so we almost always *estimate* the size of a population.

To make an estimate, we count the numbers of organisms in a *sample* of the population. A sample is a subset of the population. For the estimate to be reliable, the sample should be representative of the population as a whole.

We cannot *choose* a sample, because that would introduce **bias**. The bias would be towards our opinion of what a typical sample would be. The sample should, therefore, be a **random sample**.

The numbers of any one species in an ecosystem can be estimated using:
- **quadrats** — for relatively static organisms
- **mark–release–recapture techniques** — for animals that move further and more quickly

Changes in the distribution of species over an area are best investigated by taking regular samples along a **transect** of the area. Systematic, not random, sampling is appropriate because a random sample could omit a significant section of the transect and so would not give a true picture of change across the area.

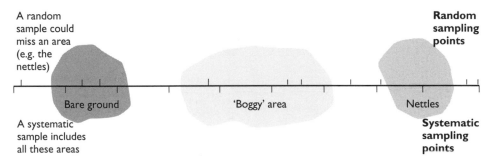

Figure 6 Systematic and random sampling along a transect

Key facts you must know and understand

Using quadrats to estimate population size
- Divide the area into a grid.

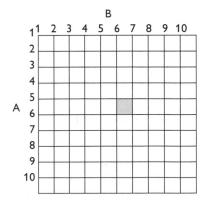

Figure 7 An area divided into a grid

- Use the random number generator on a calculator to produce a pair of coordinates, for example A5, B6 (this pair would define the top left-hand corner of the shaded square on the diagram).
- Repeat this procedure according to how many quadrats you intend to use.
- Place a quadrat with its top left-hand corner on the intersection of the coordinates.
- Count the number of organisms of the species under investigation in each sample quadrat.
- Find the mean number per quadrat.
- Find the area of the quadrat.
- Estimate the area of the field or sample area, making sure that both areas are in the same units (e.g. both in m² or both in cm²).
- Estimate the population size using the formula:

$$\frac{\text{mean number of organisms per quadrat} \times \text{area of field}}{\text{area of quadrat}}$$

If the area seems to be subdivided into regions, the above procedure can be carried out for each region, rather than for the area as a whole.

Using mark–release–recapture techniques for mobile species
- Collect a sample of the animals from the area and count them (N_1).
- Put a small mark in an unobtrusive place on each animal.
- Release them and allow time for them to disperse among the population.
- Collect a second sample and note both the total size of the sample (N_2) and the number that are marked (n).
- Estimate the population size using the formula $\dfrac{N_1 \times N_2}{n}$

For example, if 50 woodlice were originally caught, marked and released, then later 40 were caught of which 10 were marked, the population would be estimated at $(50 \times 40)/10 = 200$.

Looked at another way, in the second sample of 40, 10 (a quarter) were marked, so we assume that one-quarter of the entire population is marked. So 50 (the number originally marked) represents a quarter of the population. The population is therefore 200.

When using this technique it is assumed that:
- there are no migrations
- there is no reproduction
- there are no deaths
- there is random mixing of the marked and unmarked individuals
- marking does not affect behaviour

Using quadrats to show changes in species abundance across an area
The method is outlined below.
- Lay a tape measure across the sample area.

- At regular intervals (every 4 m in the diagram) lay five quadrats to one side (always the same side) of the tape (see Figure 8).

Tape measure

1 2 3 4 5 6 7 8 9 10 11 12 13 14 15 16 17 18 19 20 21 22 23 24

Five quadrats

Figure 8 A belt transect

- Estimate the abundance of the different organisms at each sampling point along the transect by one of the following methods:
  - counting the numbers of each organism in each quadrat to obtain a mean for each sampling point
  - calculating the **percentage frequency** of occurrence; this is done by recording presence or absence in each of the five quadrats and converting the number of occurrences to a percentage (e.g. a species that occurs in four out of five quadrats has a frequency of 80%)
  - calculating the **percentage cover**; this is done either by making a crude estimate of the percentage of each quadrat covered by the species or by using a quadrat that is subdivided into smaller squares — a 'gridded' quadrat

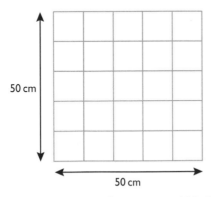

50 cm

50 cm

This quadrat has 25 small squares. Each square represents $1/25$ or 4% of the total area.

Figure 9 A gridded quadrat

If the organism covers 7 squares, the percentage cover is 7 × 4% = 28%.

If the organism covers 8 squares and 2 part-squares, a total of 9 squares is a reasonable estimate. This would give 9 × 4% = 36% cover.

These quadrats can also be used to estimate frequency. Suppose an organism occurs in 12 of the 25 squares (the actual number in each small square does not matter). The frequency of occurrence is:

$$\frac{12 \times 100}{25} = 48\%$$

Human populations

Key concepts you must understand

Any change in the size of the human population is a result of the difference between numbers born and numbers dying. There are three possibilities:

- the number of babies born exceeds the number of people dying; the population increases
- the number born is fewer than the number dying; the population decreases
- the number born equals the number dying; the population remains the same

Change in population size is usually expressed as a **population growth rate** or **rate of natural increase**. This is determined from:

- **birth rate**: the number of births per 10 000 people
- **death rate**: the number of deaths per 10 000 people

Growth rate (rate of natural increase) = birth rate – death rate

Worked example 1

Suppose the birth rate is 14 per 10 000 and the death rate is 8 per 10 000.

The population growth rate is 14 – 8 = 6 per 10 000 or +0.06%.

The population is increasing.

Worked example 2

Suppose the birth rate is 14 per 10 000 and the death rate is 16 per 10 000.

The population growth rate is 14 – 16 = –2 per 10 000 or –0.02%.

The population is decreasing.

Changes in birth and death rates expressed graphically can be used to decide whether a population is growing, shrinking or remaining static, as shown for Mexico and Sweden in Figure 10.

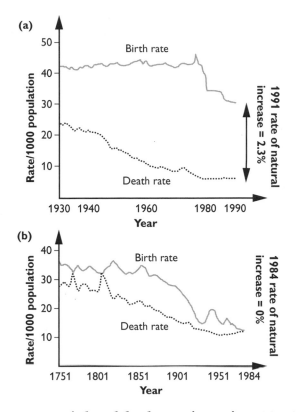

Figure 10 (a) Birth and death rates in Mexico 1930–1990
(b) Birth and death rates in Sweden 1751–1984

In Mexico:
- birth rate is always higher than death rate, so the population is increasing
- both birth rate and death rate are falling, but birth rate is falling more slowly
- the gap between birth and death rates is getting wider
- the rate of natural increase (population growth rate) is increasing

In Sweden:
- for most of the time, the birth rate is higher than death rate, so the population increased for most of the time
- both birth rate and death rate are falling, but birth rate is falling faster
- the gap between birth and death rates is getting narrower, and is zero in 1984
- the rate of natural increase (population growth rate) is decreasing and is zero in 1984: at this point the population remains the same size

Tip Be careful not to confuse population size with population growth rate. In the example about Sweden above, although the population growth *rate* (rate of natural increase) is decreasing, the population *size* increases until the growth rate is zero.

Most populations are restricted in size by **limiting factors** in the environment (see Figure 11a). Humans have been able to modify their environment and this has allowed the population to grow rapidly for the past 200 years (see Figure 11b).

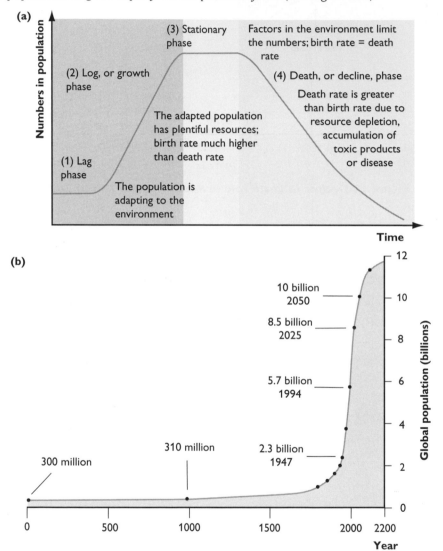

Figure 11 (a) The growth phases of a population
(b) The growth of the human population over the past 2000 years together
with the projected growth for the next 200 years

The human population has been increasing ever more rapidly for the past 200 years. This is because the death rate has declined as a result of:
- increased quality and quantity of food available
- improved sanitation
- improved medical care

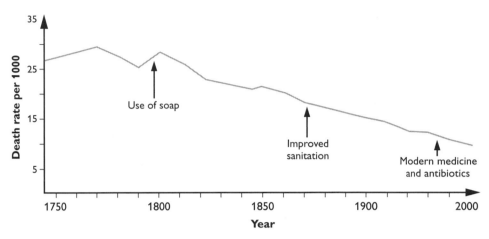

Figure 12 Decline in death rate in Sweden from 1750 to 2000

Figure 12 shows that modern medicine and antibiotics have had less impact on death rates than the use of soap and improved sanitation. Prevention is always better than cure.

Key facts you must know and understand

Biotic and abiotic factors influence human population growth and, at some point, the human population will be restricted by shortage of food or some other factor.

Human populations are subject to other factors affecting their development. These include the point at which a particular population develops agriculture and, later, becomes an industrial society. These changes affect growth rate, death rate and life expectancy. The changes are called the **demographic transition**, the four stages of which are shown in Figure 13.

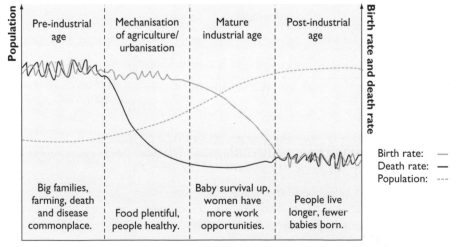

Figure 13 The stages of the demographic transition

In the second and third stages of the demographic transition death rates fall before birth rates and so the population still increases. In the final stage, birth rate and death rates are low and the population is stable.

Most developed countries are in this final stage of the demographic transition; developing countries are in one of the two middle stages. As a result, most population growth is occurring in developing countries.

In the demographic transition, the relative number of young and old people changes. These changes are best shown in **age pyramids**. Figure 14 shows age pyramids for rapidly expanding populations, slowly expanding populations, stable populations and declining populations.

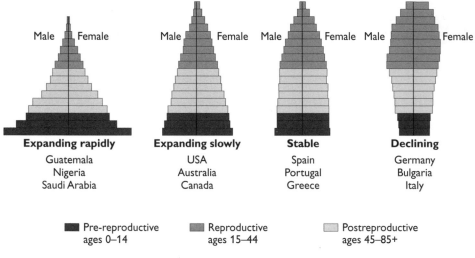

Figure 14 Age pyramids

A broad base to a population shows that large numbers of children are being born and that the population is increasing. This structure is common in developing countries.

Similar numbers in all the age groups until old age is reached shows that the number being born is approximately equal to those dying and the population is stable. This is true of many developed countries, where life expectancy is also greater.

What the examiners could ask you to do

- Explain any of the key concepts.
- Recall and show understanding of any of the key facts.
- Interpret data in graphs and tables that show change in population numbers related to changes in biotic and abiotic factors.

- Calculate estimates of population size based on data obtained from:
  - random quadrats
  - mark–release–recapture techniques
- Interpret data concerning distribution of organisms along a transect.
- Interpret data from age pyramids and make predictions as to whether the population is increasing, decreasing or stable.
- Interpret data concerning birth rates and death rates to identify stages in the demographic transition.

The transfer of energy within organisms
The structure of ATP

Key concepts you must understand

ATP is short for **a**denosine **tri**phosphate. A molecule of ATP has three components:
- adenine (one of the nitrogenous bases found in DNA and RNA)
- ribose (the sugar found in RNA)
  (The combination of adenine and ribose is called adenosine.)
- three phosphate groups

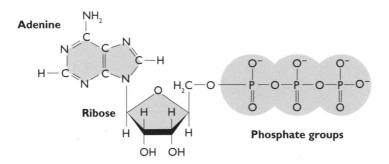

Figure 15 Structure of ATP

The third (outermost) phosphate group can be split off from the rest of the molecule. When this happens, energy is released that can be used to do useful work in the cell. Splitting off the third phosphate produces ADP (adenosine diphosphate) and P_i (inorganic phosphate). This one-step reaction is catalysed by the enzyme **ATPase**.

ADP and P_i can be joined again to make ATP, which requires an *input* of energy.

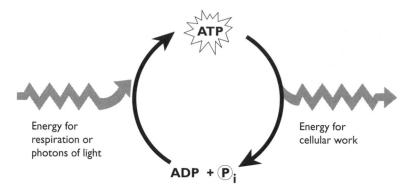

Figure 16 The interconversion of ATP, ADP and P_i

The energy required to synthesise ATP from ADP and P_i can come from:
- respiration
- the transduction of light energy in photosynthesis

Key facts you must know and understand

The main ways in which the energy released by the hydrolysis of ATP is used are shown in Figure 17.

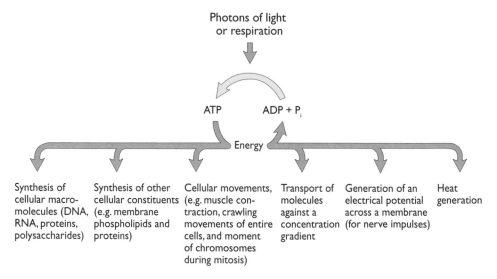

Figure 17 Uses of energy from ATP

ATP is the molecule that releases energy to drive biological processes. It is said to be **coupled** to these processes. It is an ideal molecule for this function because:

- energy is released from the molecule quickly, in a single-step hydrolysis reaction
- energy is released in small amounts that are matched closely to the amounts needed for cellular reactions
- the molecule is moved around easily within the cell, but cannot leave the cell

Photosynthesis: harnessing light energy

Key concepts you must understand

Photosynthesis is a process with two main stages: the **light-dependent reactions** and the **light-independent reactions**:

- In the light-dependent reactions, light energy is absorbed by pigments (that include **chlorophyll**) in the **chloroplasts** and is used to synthesise the high-energy molecules ATP and **reduced NADP**.
- In the light-independent reactions, the ATP and reduced NADP from the light-dependent reactions are used to drive reactions that result in the synthesis of glucose.

NADP can act as a hydrogen carrier. When it accepts hydrogen ions we say it has been reduced.

> **Tip** NADP behaves in much the same way as NAD does in respiration, but dont mix up the two molecules in your answers: NAD**P** is used in **p**hotosynthesis.

In the light-independent reactions, ATP and reduced NADP are used in the following ways:

- ATP supplies energy to drive **endergonic** (energy-requiring) reactions.
- Reduced NADP gives up its hydrogen ions, which are used to reduce another compound, GP.

The structure of chloroplasts allows the two stages of photosynthesis to occur efficiently (see Figure 18 on p.28). Chlorophyll and other light-absorbing pigments are organised into **photosystems** on the membranes of structures called **thylakoids**. This maximises the ability of the pigments to absorb light energy. The thylakoids are stacked into structures called **grana** (singular **granum**).

In the photosystems, energy from **photons** of light is transferred to a central chlorophyll molecule called the **reaction-centre** molecule (see Figure 19). The reaction-centre molecule is linked to an **electron acceptor**, which can accept high-energy electrons from the chlorophyll. Together they form the **reaction centre**.

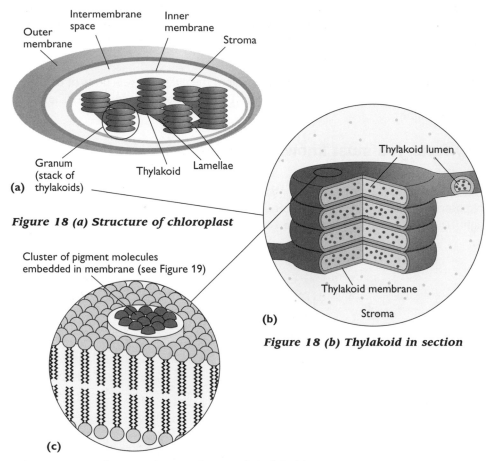

Figure 18 (a) Structure of chloroplast

Figure 18 (b) Thylakoid in section

Figure 18 (c) Pigments in membrane of thylakoid

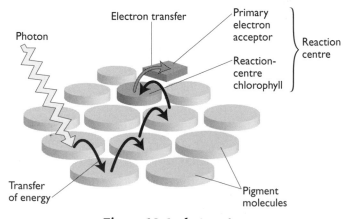

Figure 19 A photosystem

The electron acceptor transfers high-energy electrons from the chlorophyll to a chain of molecules called an **electron transfer chain**. As the electrons pass along the electron transfer chain, they lose energy, which is used to synthesise ATP (from ADP and P_i) or reduced NADP (NADPH).

Outside the thylakoids is a liquid **stroma** where the chemical reactions of the light-independent stage take place. Many chemical reactions take place most efficiently in a fluid medium.

Key facts you must know and understand

The light-dependent reactions
The light-dependent reactions take place in the **grana**. There are two different types of photosystems in the membranes of the grana that absorb different wavelengths of light. They are called **photosystem I** and **photosystem II**.

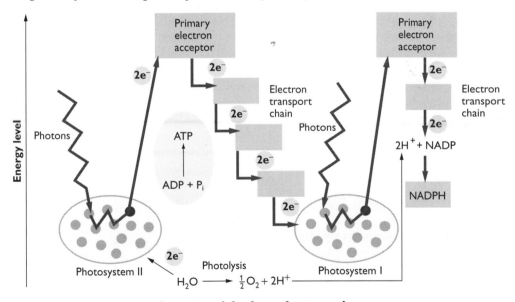

Figure 20 Light-dependent reactions

- Water molecules are split into hydrogen ions, electrons and oxygen atoms that combine to form molecular oxygen, which leaves the chloroplast.
- A chlorophyll molecule accepts the electrons.
- Light energy is absorbed by pigments in photosystem II and passed to chlorophyll in the reaction centre.
- Electrons in the chlorophyll molecule are excited (raised to a higher energy level) and escape from the chlorophyll molecule.
- The electrons are accepted by the electron acceptor and then passed along the electron transport chain. As they pass along the chain they lose energy, which is used to generate ATP.
- The electrons are transferred to chlorophyll in photosystem I.

- When energy is transferred from other pigments to the reaction centre chlorophyll in photosystem I, the electrons are excited again and escape from this chlorophyll molecule.
- The electrons are accepted by a different electron acceptor and then passed along a second electron transport chain.
- At the end of this second electron transport chain, the electrons react with hydrogen ions (supplied by the water) and NADP to form reduced NADP (NADPH).
- The ATP and NADPH leave the granum.

The light-independent reactions

These take place in the stroma.

- Carbon dioxide enters the stroma and reacts with **ribulose bisphosphate (RuBP)**, which has five carbon atoms. Two molecules of glycerate 3-phosphate (GP), which has three carbon atoms, are formed. The reaction is catalysed by the enzyme **Rubisco**.
- ATP and reduced NADP from the light-dependent reactions in the grana convert GP into triose phosphate (TP), which also has three carbon atoms; the reaction is a reduction reaction:
  - ATP supplies the energy to 'drive' the reaction
  - reduced NADP supplies the hydrogen ions for the reduction
- Some of the TP is used to synthesise hexose (6-carbon) sugars and, from them, starch and other organic compounds (such as cellulose, amino acids and lipids).
- The rest of the TP is used to resynthesise RuBP.
- ADP and NADP leave the stroma and enter the granum.

For every six turns of the cycle, six molecules of RuBP generate 12 molecules of TP. Ten of these are used to resynthesise the six RuBP molecules, leaving a 'profit' of two TP. These two TP molecules are converted into one molecule of hexose.

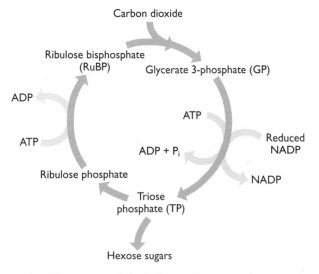

Figure 21 Light-independent reactions

Factors that can limit the rate of photosynthesis

Key concepts you must understand

The main factors that influence the rate of photosynthesis and the way in which they influence the rate are shown in the table below.

Factor	Influence on the rate of photosynthesis
Light intensity	Light energy 'drives' the light-dependent reactions. Increasing the intensity of light increases the rate of these reactions.
Carbon dioxide concentration	Carbon dioxide is needed to react with RuBP in the light-independent reactions. Increasing the concentration of carbon dioxide increases the rate of these reactions.
Temperature	Many of the reactions of photosynthesis are controlled by enzymes. Increasing the temperature to the optimum temperature for the enzymes increases the rate of photosynthesis. Above this temperature, enzymes will start to denature and the process will quickly slow down.

When several factors influence the rate of a process, their effects combine and the factor that is present in the 'least quantity' has the most influence on the overall rate. It is the **limiting factor**.

Examples of limiting factors

On a bright sunny day in January, with a temperature of +1°C, the low temperature probably limits the rate of photosynthesis. The enzymes are working well below their optimum temperature.

On a bright, sunny day in July, with a temperature of +28°C, the concentration of carbon dioxide may limit the rate of photosynthesis. The light intensity is high, and the temperature is close to the optimum for most plant enzymes in temperate countries. With more carbon dioxide, the process would probably proceed faster.

If light intensity is the factor that limits the rate of photosynthesis, then increasing the light intensity will increase the rate of photosynthesis. Increasing the concentration of carbon dioxide (when light is limiting) will have no effect.

- Increasing a non-limiting factor has no effect on the rate of photosynthesis.
- Increasing a limiting factor increases the rate of photosynthesis until the factor becomes non-limiting; then the rate will remain constant as some other factor is now limiting the rate (see Figure 22 on p.32).

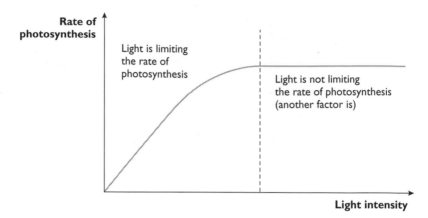

Figure 22 Effect of increasing light intensity on the rate of photosynthesis

If we now introduce the effect of carbon dioxide concentration as well as light intensity, the two factors interact as shown in Figure 23.

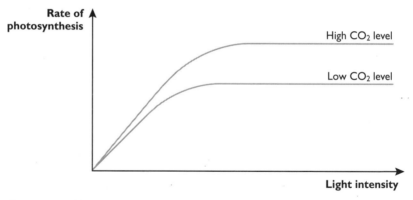

Figure 23 Effect of light intensity on the rate of photosynthesis at two different carbon dioxide levels

Both lines have the same basic shape, and light eventually becomes non-limiting in both. The point at which this happens is different because when more carbon dioxide is available, increasing the light intensity allows an even faster reaction.

Finally, consider the graph in Figure 24. It shows the same effects as the previous graph, but at two different temperatures.

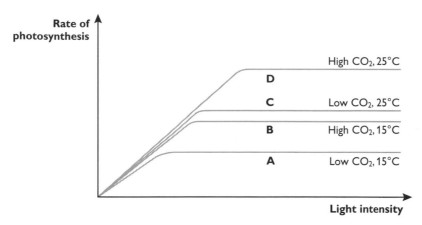

Figure 24 Effect of light intensity on the rate of photosynthesis at two different carbon dioxide concentrations at two different temperatures

In the region of the graphs where light is non-limiting (horizontal lines), the factors that are limiting are:

- **A** — both temperature and carbon dioxide; increasing either produces an increase in the rate of photosynthesis to level **B** or **C**
- **B** — temperature (the factor that hasn't been increased from **A**); increasing the temperature increases the rate to level **D**
- **C** — carbon dioxide (the factor that hasn't been increased from **A**); increasing the carbon dioxide concentration increases the rate to level **D**

Key facts you must know and understand

Increasing the temperature increases the rate of photosynthesis until it becomes limiting. After a certain point, increasing the temperature decreases the rate, as the enzymes controlling the reactions start to denature (see Figure 25 on p.34).

Growing crops in large greenhouses (glasshouses) allows the environment to be controlled to enhance photosynthesis and so increase productivity (see Figure 26 on p.34).

The greenhouse effect happens in greenhouses as well as in the Earth's atmosphere. Short-wave radiation entering becomes longer-wave radiation as it strikes a surface in the greenhouse. This cannot escape as easily, so the greenhouse warms up.

Growers can increase the temperature inside a greenhouse by burning a fossil fuel. This also increases the concentration of carbon dioxide in the air in the greenhouse. Two potentially limiting factors are increased at the same time. However, growers will take care not to overheat the greenhouse because it will cost extra money for no extra return (see Figure 27 on p.35).

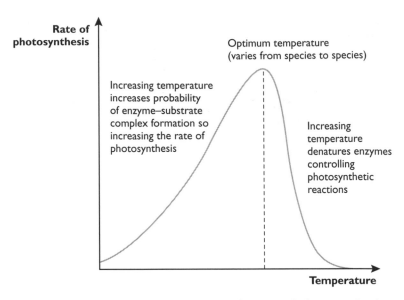

Figure 25 Effect of temperature on the rate of photosynthesis

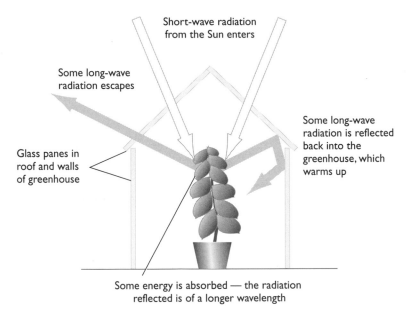

Figure 26 Greenhouse effect

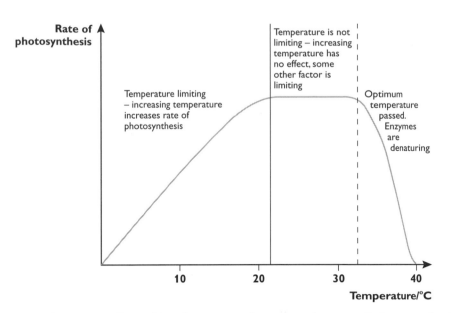

Figure 27 Effect of heating a greenhouse on the rate of photosynthesis

In this example, there is no point in the grower heating the greenhouse above 22°C as it would produce no further increase in the rate of photosynthesis.

What the examiners could ask you to do

- Explain any of the key concepts.
- Recall and show understanding of any of the key facts.
- Relate the structure of a chloroplast to its function in photosynthesis.
- Complete diagrams showing the main reactions of photosynthesis. You may have to name compounds or state the number of carbon atoms a molecule of a particular compound contains.
- Interpret graphs showing the effects on the rate of photosynthesis of changing one or more of the factors that affect the process.
- Relate the influence of environmental factors that affect photosynthesis to conditions maintained in a greenhouse.
- Link photosynthesis to transfer of energy along food chains.
- Link the rate of photosynthesis to productivity of an area.

Respiration: releasing energy from organic molecules

Key concepts you must understand

Respiration *releases* energy from organic molecules.

> **Tip** Take care not to say that respiration *produces* energy. ATP is produced, storing the energy that is *released* from the organic molecules.

There are two kinds of respiration:
- **aerobic respiration**, which requires the presence of oxygen
- **anaerobic respiration**, which can take place in the absence of oxygen

In both processes, molecules are **dehydrogenated** (hydrogen atoms are removed). These hydrogen atoms are used to reduce **NAD** (a molecule that is similar to the NADP used in photosynthesis) to form **reduced NAD**. In aerobic respiration, a similar molecule, **FAD**, is also reduced to form **reduced FAD**.

Some of the ATP produced in aerobic respiration and all of the ATP produced in anaerobic respiration is produced by **substrate-level phosphorylation**. In this process, a phosphorylated substance (a substance with a phosphate group attached; XP in the equation below) transfers its phosphate group to ADP, producing a molecule of ATP.

$$XP + ADP \xrightarrow{\text{Substrate-level phosphorylation}} X + ATP$$

Aerobic respiration

Key concepts you must understand

In aerobic respiration, most ATP is produced when hydrogen ions (H^+) move through a molecule called **ATP synthase** (see Figure 28). This can be thought of as a molecular water wheel. As the hydrogen ions pass through the molecule, they make part of the molecule spin. The energy of the spinning molecule allows ATP to be produced from ADP and P_i. The ATP synthase molecules are located in the inner membrane of the mitochondrion.

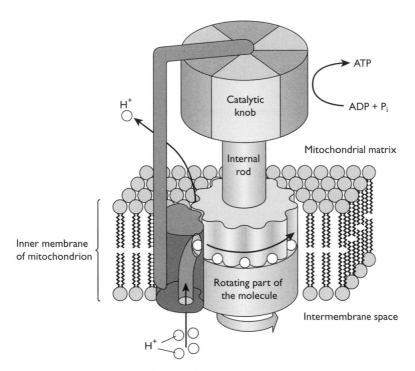

Figure 28 ATP synthase

Key facts you must know and understand

Most of the ATP-producing reactions of aerobic respiration occur inside the mitochondria. Some occur in the matrix of the mitochondrion, but most ATP is formed by the ATP synthase in the inner membrane of the mitochondrion.

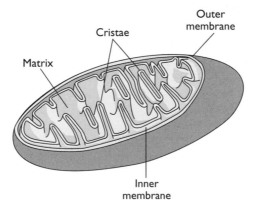

Figure 29 Structure of a mitochondrion

The respiratory substrates (the substances that are respired, such as glucose and fatty acids) cannot enter a mitochondrion. In the early reactions of aerobic respiration, they are converted into a molecule called **pyruvate**. This molecule *can* enter a mitochondrion.

There are four stages in the aerobic respiration of glucose as illustrated in Figure 30.

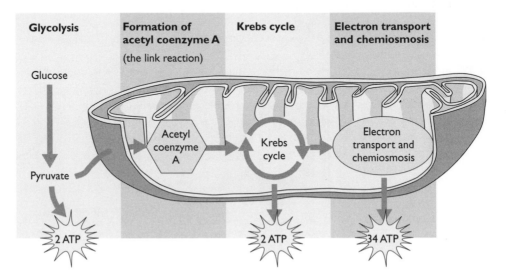

Figure 30 Outline of the stages of aerobic respiration

Glycolysis

Glycolysis occurs in the cytoplasm. It is a series of reactions in which glucose is converted into pyruvate:

- Two molecules of ATP are used to 'energise' the glucose molecule and 'kick-start' the process.
- The glucose molecule is split into two molecules of GP (each containing three carbon atoms).
- Each molecule of GP is converted into a molecule of pyruvate.
- Four molecules of ATP are produced (per molecule of glucose) giving a net yield of 2 ATP per molecule of glucose.
- Two molecules of reduced NAD are also generated (per molecule of glucose).

The link reaction

Pyruvate formed in glycolysis moves into the mitochondrion where it is converted into **acetyl CoA**. The reaction occurs in the matrix of the mitochondrion.

In the link reaction, each pyruvate molecule loses:

- a carbon atom (it is **decarboxylated**) and a molecule of carbon dioxide is formed
- hydrogen atoms (it is **dehydrogenated**), which are accepted by NAD to form one molecule of reduced NAD.

So, because two molecules of pyruvate are produced per molecule of glucose, the link reaction produces per molecule of glucose:

- two molecules of acetyl CoA (each containing two carbon atoms)
- two molecules of carbon dioxide
- two molecules of reduced NAD

The Krebs cycle

In this series of reactions, which occur in the matrix of the mitochondrion:

- Acetyl CoA reacts with a four-carbon compound (oxaloacetate) to form a six-carbon compound (citrate).
- Citrate loses a carbon atom to become a five-carbon compound (α-ketoglutarate).
- α-ketoglutarate loses a carbon atom to reform oxaloacetate.
- Hydrogen atoms are lost and are used to reduce NAD and FAD.

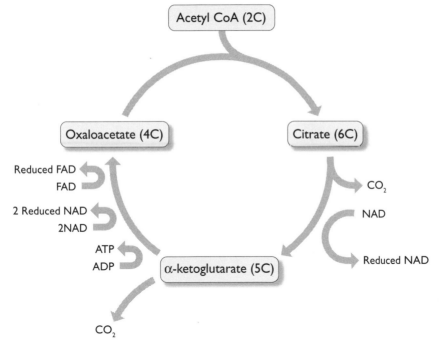

Figure 31 Krebs cycle

One 'turn' of the Krebs cycle produces:

- one molecule of ATP by substrate-level phosphorylation (two per molecule of glucose)
- three molecules of reduced NAD (six per molecule of glucose)
- one molecule of reduced FAD (similar to NAD) (two per molecule of glucose)
- two molecules of carbon dioxide (four per molecule of glucose)

Reduced NAD and reduced FAD supply hydrogen ions (to drive the ATP synthase) and high-energy electrons that are used to power hydrogen pumps in the electron transport chain.

Electron transport and chemiosmosis

The molecules of the electron transport chain are built into the inner membrane of the mitochondrion, like the molecules of ATP synthase.

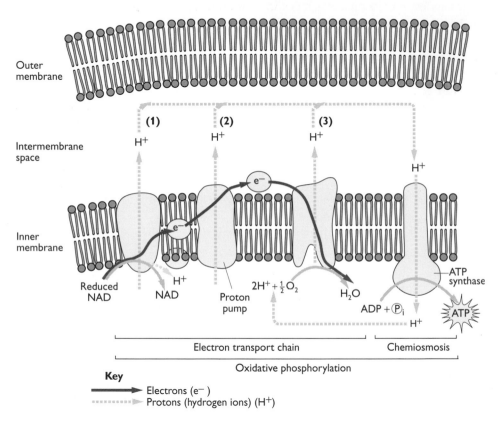

Figure 32 Electron transport and chemiosmosis

The electron transport chain

- Reduced NAD binds with the first proton pump and hydrogen atoms are released.
- These split into hydrogen ions (protons) and electrons.
- The electrons are accepted by the proton pump and then transferred to the next component in the chain.
- The loss of energy in this transfer of the electron 'powers' the pumping of a hydrogen ion (proton) through the pump into the space between the two mitochondrial membranes (the intermembrane space).
- As electrons flow along the chain they lose further energy, which is used to power the pumping of hydrogen ions through proton pumps 2 and 3.

- At the end of the chain, the electrons combine with hydrogen ions and oxygen to form water.
- Since oxygen is the last substance to 'accept' the electrons, it is called the **terminal electron acceptor**.

The chemiosmotic synthesis of ATP

- As the electrons from a reduced NAD (NADH) molecule pass along the transport chain, they move three hydrogen ions through the proton pumps.
- The continual pumping of hydrogen ions into the intermembrane space creates a hydrogen ion gradient between the intermembrane space and the matrix.
- This gradient results in hydrogen ions moving through ATP synthase.
- When a hydrogen ion moves through ATP synthase, it causes one molecule of ATP to be synthesised.
- Electrons from a molecule of reduced FAD (FADH) only move two hydrogen ions through the proton pumps and so only two molecules of ATP are synthesised.

The formation of ATP by chemiosmosis depends on the electron transport chain transferring electrons to create the hydrogen ion gradient. Without oxygen to accept the electrons at the end of the chain, the electron transfer and hydrogen ion pumping would cease. Because it depends on oxygen, this method of producing ATP is called **oxidative phosphorylation**.

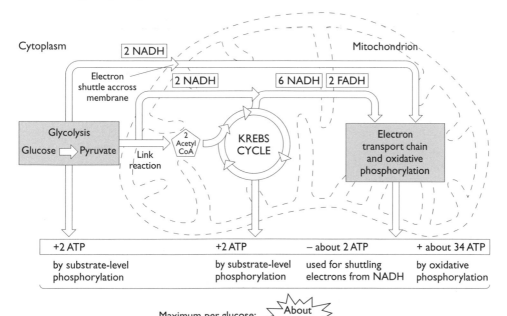

Figure 33 The production of ATP from glucose in aerobic respiration

Anaerobic respiration

Key concepts you must understand

In the absence of oxygen, the electron transport chain cannot take place because oxygen is not present to act as the terminal electron acceptor. As a result:
- there is a build up of reduced NAD and reduced FAD because they cannot be re-oxidised
- the link reaction and Krebs cycle cannot take place

Glycolysis continues because:
- reduced NAD is used to reduce pyruvate (formed in glycolysis) to either lactate (animals) or ethanol (plants and yeast)
- at the same time, reduced NAD is oxidised to NAD
- enough NAD is formed in this way to maintain the reactions of glycolysis

Because only glycolysis (plus the reduction of pyruvate) takes place, anaerobic respiration is much less efficient than aerobic respiration. Each molecule of glucose yields only two molecules of ATP compared with the 36 ATP molecules generated by the aerobic pathway.

Key facts you must know and understand

In anaerobic respiration:
- Glucose is converted to pyruvate by glycolysis.
- The net yield of ATP is two molecules per molecule of glucose.
- ATP is only generated by substrate-level phosphorylation during glycolysis.
- The reduced NAD generated cannot pass electrons down the electron transport chain because there is no oxygen to accept them.
- Reduced NAD is used to reduce pyruvate to either ethanol or lactate. This makes NAD available again and allows the glycolysis reactions to continue.

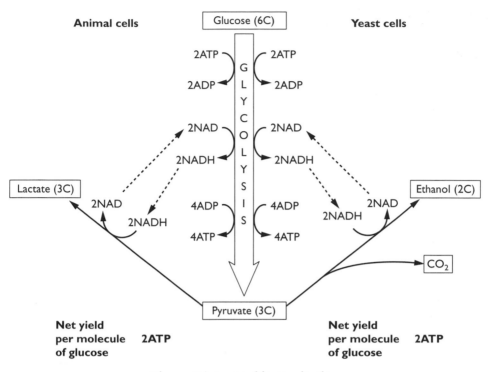

Figure 34 Anaerobic respiration

What the examiners could ask you to do

- Explain any of the key concepts.
- Recall and show understanding of any of the key facts.
- Relate the structure of a mitochondrion to its function in respiration.
- Explain the importance of the regeneration of NAD in anaerobic respiration.
- Calculate the ATP yield from the various stages of aerobic respiration.
- Complete diagrams showing the main reactions of respiration. You may have to name compounds or state the number of carbon atoms a compound contains.
- Explain the significance of anaerobic respiration (lactate fermentation) in animal cells.
- Relate the release of energy in respiration to energy-requiring processes, including those described in the AS course.
- Explain the importance of anaerobic respiration (alcoholic fermentation) in yeast.

The transfer of energy between organisms
The transfer of energy through ecosystems

Key concepts you must understand

Energy cannot be created or destroyed. It can only be transferred and, in the transfer, converted from one form to another. This is called the **conservation of energy**.

The amount of usable energy in a biological system decreases as energy is transferred.

- Energy enters ecosystems as light and is transduced to chemical energy in the biological molecules that plants produce as a result of photosynthesis.
- Some of the chemical energy in these biological molecules is transferred to animals when they feed.
- Some of the energy in the biological molecules of plants is released in respiration and is used to drive other processes in the plant and is then lost as heat.
- The same is true when carnivorous animals eat other animals and when decomposers break down dead remains.

Energy can only be used once by an organism. Energy that is used to contract a muscle cannot be used later in the active transport of ions. This is because in using the energy, it becomes transduced to heat. In this form, the energy cannot be used to create ATP.

The transfer of energy through ecosystems can be represented in food chains, food webs, pyramids of numbers, pyramids of biomass and energy flow diagrams.

Key facts you must know and understand

The biological molecules an organism takes in are used in one of two main ways:

- They are respired to produce ATP, which is used to drive processes such as muscle contraction and active transport; the energy is then lost as heat
- They are assimilated into the structure of the organism; the energy in the molecules remains within the organism.

Energy is transferred from one organism to another by feeding. This is represented in a **food chain** — for example:

Grass → Gazelle → Cheetah

The processes involved in the transfer of energy are as follows:

- Light energy enters the grass (the **producer**).
- In photosynthesis, the light energy is transduced to chemical energy in organic molecules, such as glucose.

- Some of these chemicals are used in growth to build new cells (assimilation) and are retained within the grass.
- Some are used in respiration and, once used, the energy released is lost as heat.
- The gazelle (**primary consumer**) eats and digests some of the grass, transferring chemical energy to its cells in the organic molecules it absorbs.
- Some of these chemicals are used in growth to build new cells (assimilation) and are retained within the gazelle.
- Some are used in respiration and, once used, the energy released is lost as heat.
- The cheetah (**secondary consumer**) eats and digests parts of the gazelle, transferring chemical energy to its cells in the organic molecules it absorbs.
- Some of these chemicals are used in growth to build new cells (assimilation) and are retained within the cheetah.
- Some are used in respiration and, once used, the energy released is lost as heat.
- At each stage in the food chain, organisms that are not eaten eventually die and chemical energy contained in their cells is transferred during decay to **decomposers** in the organic molecules they absorb from the dead organisms.
- Some of these chemicals are used to build new cells and are assimilated into the decomposers.
- Some are used in respiration and the energy released is lost as heat.
- The different feeding levels (producer, primary consumer, secondary consumer and decomposer) are called **trophic levels**.

The flow of energy through this simple food chain can be represented as below.

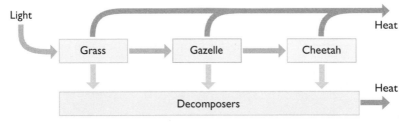

Figure 35 Flow of energy through a food chain

Food chains almost never exist in isolation, but are interlinked to form food webs (see Figure 36). Changes in the number of any organism in a food web may influence the numbers of another organism:

- In the soil food web in Figure 36a, a decrease in the number of fungi could lead to an increase in the number of protozoa as there would be more organic matter, which could lead to an increase in the numbers of bacteria, which could lead to an increase in the number of protozoa.
- In the marine food web, a decrease in the number of crabeater seals could lead to an increase in the number of petrels as there would be more fish, which could lead to an increase in the number of petrels.

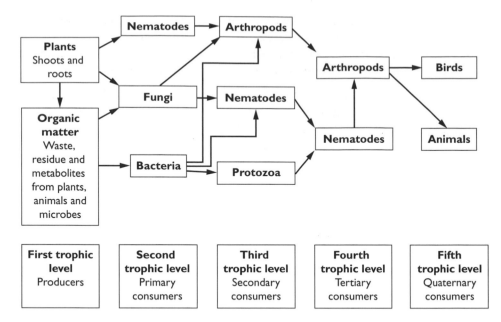

Figure 36 (a) A food web in soil

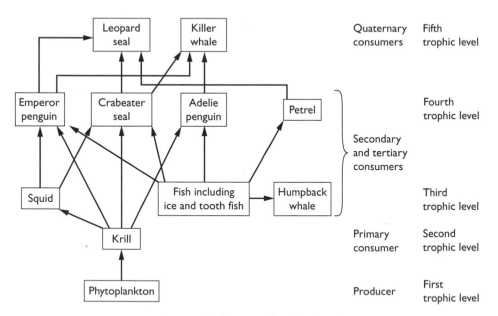

Figure 36 (b) A marine food web

The flow of energy through the food webs in different ecosystems has been measured (see Figure 37). The figures are usually expressed as the amount of energy transfer per square metre per year (for example kJ m^{-2} yr^{-1}). This then allows comparisons between different-sized ecosystems and measurements that were taken for different periods of time.

The number of trophic levels in an ecosystem does not often exceed five because:
- only a fraction of the light shining on an area is actually used in photosynthesis
- on average, only 10% of the energy in a trophic level is passed to the next level
- there is too little energy in the fifth trophic level to support another trophic level

In some regions, the density of the producers is so great that they, collectively, absorb a higher percentage of the light striking the area. This allows six or even seven trophic levels. This happens in tropical rainforest and in some areas of the oceans.

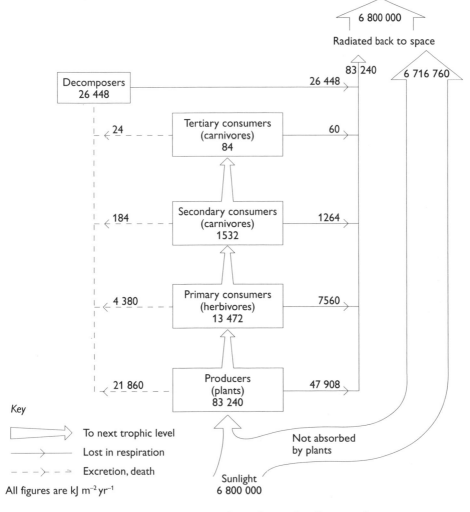

Figure 37 Energy flow through Silver Springs

Notice that energy is conserved at each trophic level. The energy entering each level is then:
- transferred to the next trophic level, or
- lost in respiration, or
- transferred to the decomposers in excretory products or in the dead bodies of the organisms

Notice also that energy is conserved in the ecosystem as a whole. All the energy entering in sunlight is eventually radiated back to space. Most is reflected off plants, but some passes through the organisms in the ecosystem before it is re-radiated.

Ecological pyramids

Key concepts you must understand

- Food chains can be represented as ecological pyramids, such as pyramids of numbers, pyramids of biomass and pyramids of energy.
- A pyramid of numbers represents the total numbers of the organisms in a food chain, at a given moment, irrespective of biomass (size).
- A pyramid of biomass represents the total biomass of the organisms in a food chain, at a given moment, irrespective of numbers.
- A pyramid of energy represents the amount of energy transferred to each level of a food chain, irrespective of numbers and biomass, in a given period of time.
- Pyramids of biomass and energy can also represent the biomass or energy transfer of each trophic level in a food web.
- An energy flow diagram represents the amount of energy passing through the various levels of an ecosystem in a given period of time.

Rather than consider these concepts generally, it is helpful to think of specific examples. Think of the food chain: grass → grasshoppers → frogs → birds.

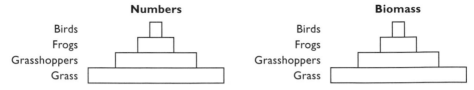

Figure 38 Pyramids representing the food chain:
grass → grasshoppers → frogs → birds

The two pyramids for this food chain look the same, as numbers and mass are related. The individual organisms increase in mass along the chain, so a decrease in biomass necessarily also means a decrease in numbers.

Think of the food chain: oak tree → aphids → ladybirds → birds.

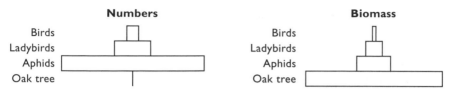

Figure 39 Pyramids representing the food chain:
oak tree → aphids → ladybirds → birds

The pyramids for this food chain are very different because of the huge biomass of just one oak tree. The *decrease in biomass* to the next stage is accompanied by an *increase in numbers*. After this, numbers and mass are related as in the first food chain.

Pyramids of numbers can be further complicated if the end consumer is parasitised. What if the birds in the second food chain were parasitised by tiny mites? Each bird would have many mites on its body and so the pyramid of numbers would now look as in Figure 40.

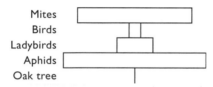

Figure 40 A pyramid of numbers when the food chain involves parasites

However, the biomass pyramid (Figure 41) is a true pyramid. Each mite has a much smaller mass than the bird and collectively they still weigh less than the birds they parasitise.

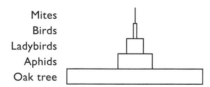

Figure 41 A pyramid of biomass when the food chain involves parasites

Key facts you must know and understand

Explaining the shape of pyramids of biomass is relatively straightforward. When a rabbit eats grass, not all of the materials in the grass plants end up as rabbit. There are losses because:
- some parts of the grass are not eaten — the roots for example
- some parts are not digested and so are not absorbed (they are lost in faeces)
- metabolism of some of the materials absorbed leads to the formation of excretory products, which are released into the environment

- many of the materials are respired to release energy: the carbon dioxide formed at the same time is exhaled

Only a small fraction of the materials in the grass becomes incorporated into new cells in the rabbit. Similar losses are repeated at each trophic level in the food chain, so a smaller amount of biomass is available for growth at successive levels. Pyramids of biomass are usually 'pyramid shaped' to reflect this. The loss in biomass at each level usually means smaller numbers. The exceptions to this occur when:

- very large producers are eaten by smaller consumers
- an organism is parasitised

What the examiners could ask you to do

- Explain any of the key concepts.
- Recall and show understanding of any of the key facts.
- Construct pyramids of numbers and biomass from data supplied.
- Analyse and explain the shapes of pyramids of numbers and biomass.
- Interpret energy flow diagrams and calculate the energy passing to various trophic levels.

Energy and food production

Key concepts you must understand

Productivity is the amount of the energy input to a trophic level that is converted into biomass:

- in a given period of time (often a year)
- for a given area of the ecosystem (often a square metre)

It may be expressed in mass units (usually kilograms) or energy units (usually kilojoules).

Plants are the producers, so their productivity is called **primary productivity**.

However, not all the biomass produced by plants in a year remains as biomass. Some is respired, and the products of respiration are lost, taking with them some of the energy fixed into biomass.

- **Gross primary productivity** (G) is all the biomass produced by the plant per m^2 per year.
- **Net primary productivity** (N) is the biomass that is left per m^2 per year, after losses in respiration (R) are taken into account. This is the biomass of the plants that will pass either to the primary consumers or to the decomposers on death of the plants.

Therefore:

N = G − R

Secondary productivity is the rate of production of biomass by animals in an ecosystem. As with primary productivity, it is measured in mass units or energy units per unit of time (usually a year) per unit of area (usually a square metre). The biomass remaining in the animals needs to take into account:

- the amount of energy ingested (C)
- the amount of cellular respiration (R)
- the amount of energy lost in urine (U)
- the amount of energy lost in faeces (F)

Therefore:

P (net secondary productivity) = C − (R + U + F)

The figures for gross and net productivities for the Silver Springs ecosystem (Figure 37, p.47) are shown in Figure 42.

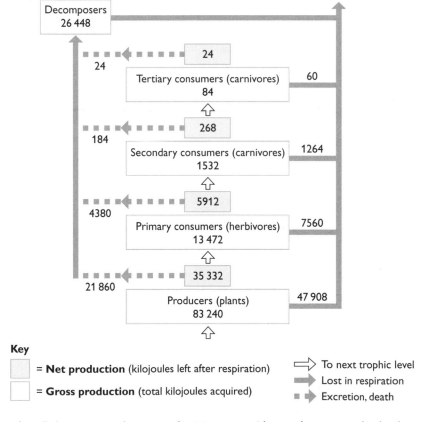

Key

☐ = **Net production** (kilojoules left after respiration)

☐ = **Gross production** (total kilojoules acquired)

⇨ To next trophic level
➡ Lost in respiration
■⇨ Excretion, death

Notice that all the energy in the net productivity passes either to the next trophic level or to the decomposers

Figure 42 Gross and net productivities in the Silver Springs ecosystem

Key facts you must know and understand

A farmer aims to get as much biomass production for as little input as possible.

In the case of crop plants, the following practices are adopted:
- monoculture
- the use of fertilisers
- the use of pesticides
- biological control
- integrated control systems
- intensive rearing of livestock

Monoculture

This means growing a single type of crop over a wide area. Monoculture allows:
- easier control of pests — the number of different pests is often limited by the crop and so specific pesticides can be used
- reduced plant competition for nutrients, space and solar radiation — only the crop plant is taking nutrients from the soil and absorbing light energy
- maximised profit from the growing of high gross margin crops

The use of fertilisers

Harvesting crop plants breaks the normal cycle of decay and mineral ions are not returned to the soil, which becomes mineral-poor. Fertilisers add mineral ions to the soil (see Figure 43).

Organic fertilisers are materials produced directly from animals, plants and other living organisms and must be decomposed to release mineral ions. They are, therefore, **slow-release** fertilisers. They include materials such as farmyard manure, seaweed, dried blood, sewage sludge and poultry manure.

Inorganic fertilisers do not need to be broken down because they are already in the form of mineral ions. They are, therefore, **quick-release** fertilisers.

Some properties of organic and inorganic fertilisers are compared in the table below.

Property	Organic fertilisers	Inorganic fertilisers
Release of ions	Slow — they must decay	Fast — they are ionic
Solubility	Low	High
Time of application	Early — applied before the crop requires the ions to allow time for decay	Late — applied as the crops approach peak demand as the ions are absorbed immediately
Consequences of overuse	Few problems because of low solubility and slow release of ions	Eutrophication — high solubility means ions are leached easily into waterways

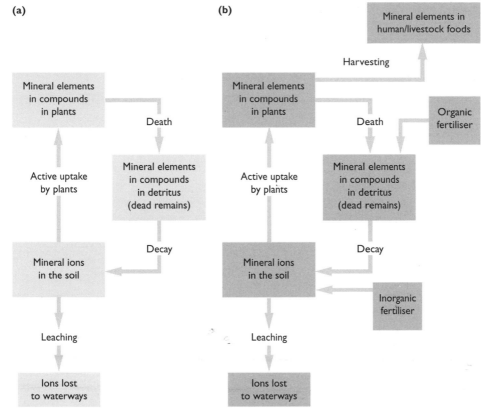

(a)

(b)

Figure 43 (a) The natural cycle
(b) The effects of harvesting and the use of fertilisers

The use of pesticides

Pests reduce the productivity of crops. Pests include animals, plants (weeds) and some fungi.

Weeds compete with crop plants for the available light, water, carbon dioxide and mineral ions. This is an example of interspecific competition (see pages 13–15). They often outcompete the crop plants because they have higher growth rates than the crops. They establish their root and shoot systems more quickly and so obtain more of the available resources, reducing their availability to the crop plants and thus reducing yields.

Insect pests can reduce the yield of the crop in a number of ways:
- They can feed directly on the organ of the plant that forms the crop.
- They can reduce the yield by feeding on the leaves; this reduces the leaf area and therefore the capacity of the plant for photosynthesis.

- They can feed on and damage the roots, restricting the uptake of mineral ions essential for growth.
- They can feed from the phloem and so disrupt the transfer of sugars manufactured in photosynthesis to other organs.
- They can spread organisms that cause disease.

A **pesticide** is a chemical that helps to control the population of a pest. Pesticides can be classified according to the type of organism they control, for example:
- **insecticides** kill insects
- **herbicides** kill plants (they are weed killers)
- **fungicides** kill fungi
- **molluscicides** kill molluscs (slugs and snails)

Some pesticides have effects on organisms in the environment other than the pests they are used to control. These effects include the following:
- Insecticides might kill useful insects as well as the targeted harmful insects.
- Some pesticides persist in the environment for many years before they are finally broken down; they may be taken up by crop plants and so enter humans through the food chain.
- Some pesticides (such as DDT) accumulate along food chains (**bioaccumulation**).

Biological control

This involves introducing a natural parasite or predator of the pest into the area. The aim is to reduce the pest population to a level that does not cause major damage.

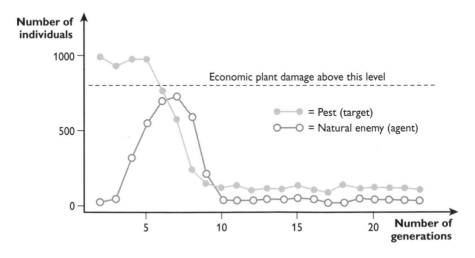

Biological control maintains the numbers of pests at a low level, but does not eradicate them

Figure 44 Biological control

Biological control methods include the following:
- Introducing a **predator** — for example, ladybirds have been used to control aphid populations in orange groves.

- Introducing a **herbivore** — for example, a moth native to South America was introduced to Australia to control the 'prickly pear' cactus.
- Introducing a **parasite** — for example, larvae of the wasp *Encarsia* parasitise whiteflies on tomato crops in greenhouses.
- Introducing **sterile males** — this reduces the number of successful matings and so reduces the pest numbers.
- Using **pheromones** — these animal sex hormones are used to attract the males or females, which are then destroyed; male-attracting pheromones are used to control the damson-hop aphid, reducing damage to plum crops.

Biological control has several advantages over the use of pesticides:

- Pests do not usually develop resistance to a predator or parasite.
- Biological control agents are usually much more specific than pesticides; for example, a carefully chosen predator will target only the pest, whereas a pesticide might target all the animals of a particular group (an insecticide might kill many kinds of insect).
- Once a natural predator or parasite has been introduced, no further reintroductions are necessary, whereas pesticides must be re-applied regularly.

Problems with biological control include the following:

- Research is necessary to ensure that the proposed control agent will control only the pest population and that the control agent will reproduce in the new conditions.
- Using biological control to reduce the numbers of one specific pest may allow another pest to fill its ecological niche.
- Biological control is not an appropriate method for controlling pests of stored grain. The grain would become contaminated with the dead bodies of pest and control agent alike.

Integrated control systems

Often, neither chemical control nor biological control alone is really effective in controlling pests. Biological control is often enhanced when low levels of pesticides are used at the same time. This is a simple example of an **integrated control system**.

In integrated crop management, most or all of the following would be considered as methods of maximising productivity:

- selecting crops that are adapted to the type of soil and the climate in the area
- selecting crops that have some resistance to known pests in the area
- choosing appropriate methods of pest control
- rotating crops grown in a particular field so that the same pests do not build up in the soil and the same ions are not continually removed by the crop
- using fertilisers (organic, inorganic or a combination) that are appropriate to the conditions, to replace the mineral ions removed by cropping
- appropriate treatment and storage of the final crop (to minimise damage by pests)
- irrigation of the soil (where necessary)

By using a combination of these techniques, a farmer can reduce damage by pests and ensure that crops have a continuous supply of mineral ions.

Intensive rearing of livestock

Traditionally, stock animals were allowed to wander where they wished, within the boundaries of fields or pens. The main principles of intensive farming practices include:

- feeding a precisely controlled diet that encourages the production of meat with little fat
- using hormone injections or supplements to increase the rate of growth
- restricting the movement of the animals so that less energy is lost this way and more energy is used in growth
- keeping the animals in a warm environment so that less energy is lost as heat to the environment and more is used in growth

What the examiners could ask you to do

- Explain any of the key concepts.
- Recall and show understanding of any of the key facts.
- Interpret data concerning energy flow through natural and farmed ecosystems and explain any differences.
- Interpret data concerning crop yields in different production methods.
- Interpret data concerning different pest control methods and explain any differences.
- Relate results from biological control experiments to the predator–prey model.

How elements are cycled in ecosystems
The carbon and nitrogen cycles

Key concepts you must understand

- Life on Earth is carbon-based; carbohydrates, lipids, proteins, nucleic acids and ATP all contain carbon.
- Proteins, nucleic acids and ATP contain nitrogen as well as carbon.

There is a fixed amount of carbon and nitrogen within an ecosystem, so these elements must be recycled.

Microorganisms in the soil decay dead organic matter. As by-products of the decay process, carbon atoms and nitrogen atoms in organic molecules are converted into forms that can be taken up and used by plants. In this way, the elements are recycled.

The levels of carbon dioxide in the atmosphere fluctuate as overall rates of photosynthesis and respiration change. In winter, the amount of photosynthesis is reduced due to:
- cooler temperatures
- shorter day length
- loss of leaves by many plants

Less carbon dioxide is absorbed from the atmosphere. Respiration may also be reduced, but it produces more carbon dioxide than is used in photosynthesis. The concentration of carbon dioxide rises. In summer, the balance is reversed and the concentration of carbon dioxide in the atmosphere falls.

The concentration of carbon dioxide in the atmosphere has remained more or less constant for millions of years due to:
- the removal of carbon dioxide from the air by plants for use in photosynthesis
- the addition of carbon dioxide to the air by all organisms as a result of respiration

The recent increase in the amount of carbon dioxide in the atmosphere is probably due to the increased combustion of fossil fuels by humans. Measurements of the concentration of carbon dioxide at Mauna Loa on Hawaii show:
- the annual fluctuations
- an overall trend of increasing concentration of carbon dioxide

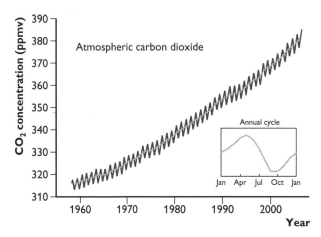

Figure 45 Changes in carbon dioxide concentrations since 1960 at Mauna Loa

Carbon dioxide is a greenhouse gas. It may be a factor in global warming by contributing to the greenhouse effect.

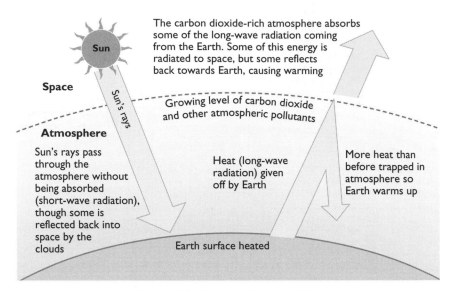

Figure 46 The greenhouse effect

However, the evidence is correlational so no definite cause and effect can be proved. It is also conflicting.

Over the past 30 years the carbon dioxide concentration has increased and so has the temperature of the Earth. However, if we look over longer periods of time, the correlation is not so clear-cut. The changes in temperature and carbon dioxide concentration since 1850 (when the industrial revolution had begun) do not always coincide.

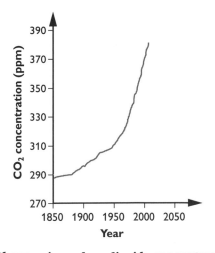

Figure 47 (a) Changes in carbon dioxide concentration since 1850

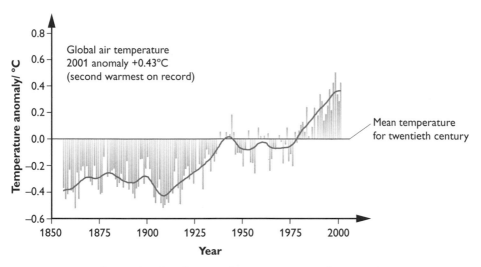

Figure 47 (b) Changes in temperature since 1850

Over a longer period than this, it seems that the correlation has returned, as shown in Figure 48:

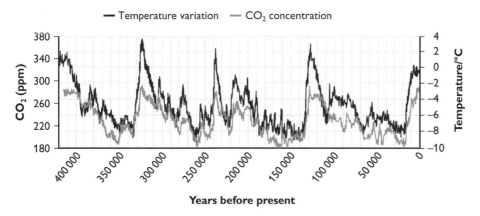

Figure 48 Changes in temperature and carbon dioxide concentration over the past 400 000 years

However, an even longer period once again reveals inconsistency.

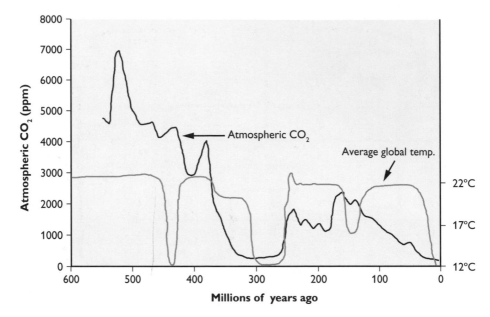

Figure 49 Changes in temperature and carbon dioxide concentrations over 600 million years

Bear in mind also that increased temperature will cause carbon dioxide dissolved in water to escape. Global warming may be causing the increase in carbon dioxide concentration.

Key facts you must know and understand

The carbon cycle

The main processes involved in cycling carbon through ecosystems are:

- photosynthesis — the process that fixes carbon atoms from carbon dioxide into organic compounds (e.g. glucose)
- feeding and assimilation — feeding passes carbon atoms in organic molecules to the next trophic level in the food chain where they are assimilated into (become part of) the body of that organism
- respiration — this releases carbon dioxide from organic compounds
- fossilisation — sometimes dead material does not decay fully due to the conditions in the soil, and fossil fuels (e.g. coal, oil and peat) are formed
- combustion — fossil fuels are burned, releasing carbon dioxide into the atmosphere

Figure 50 summarises the carbon cycle.

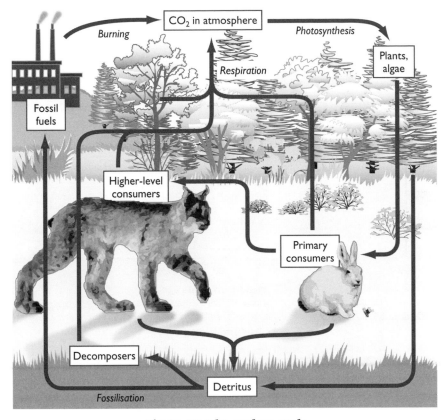

Figure 50 The carbon cycle

The nitrogen cycle

The main processes in the nitrogen cycle are:

- Plants absorb nitrates from the soil.
- Plants use the nitrates and compounds from respiration to form amino acids.
- The amino acids are used to synthesise proteins.
- The plants are eaten by animals, the proteins digested into amino acids; the amino acids are absorbed and assimilated into animal proteins.
- Both plants and animals die, leaving a collection of dead materials (detritus) which contain the nitrogen still fixed in organic molecules.
- Decomposers decay the excretory products and detritus, releasing ammonia (NH_3) into the soil.
- Nitrifying bacteria oxidise the ammonia first to nitrites (NO_2^-), then to nitrates (NO_3^-), which are taken up by the plants.

In addition to these processes, nitrogen-fixing bacteria living free in the soil and in nodules on the roots of legumes (plants with 'pods' such as peas, beans, lentils and clover) 'fix' nitrogen gas into molecules of ammonia. This adds to the total amount of nitrogen available for use by the plants.

Denitrifying bacteria reduce nitrate to nitrogen gas that escapes from the soil. This decreases the total amount of nitrogen available to the plants.

Figure 51 summarises the biological nitrogen cycle.

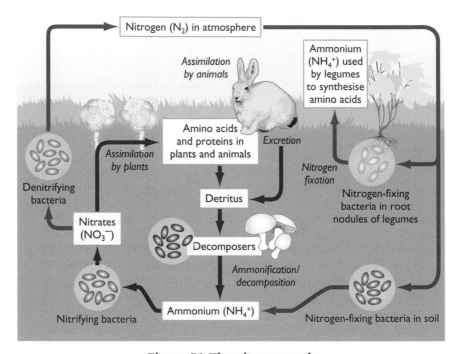

Figure 51 The nitrogen cycle

Too much nitrogen: eutrophication

When inorganic fertilisers are used, mineral ions are added directly to the soil and are available instantly. Because these ions are soluble (particularly nitrates and phosphates), they can be carried into nearby waterways. This is called **leaching**.

If inorganic fertilisers are overused, too many nitrate ions are leached and the following can happen:

- Algae in the waterway multiply rapidly because increased synthesis of proteins and nucleic acids is possible.
- The increased algal growth forms a mat over the surface (if the algae are filamentous) or algal bloom (if the algae are unicellular).
- The algal mat or bloom reduces the transmission of light to lower levels of the waterway.
- Plants growing at these levels cannot photosynthesise and so they die.
- Algae also start to die as the mineral ions are used up.
- Microorganisms decompose the dead plants and algae and reproduce rapidly as more and more algae and plants die.

- The microorganisms use up oxygen in aerobic respiration in increasing amounts as their numbers increase.
- The concentration of oxygen in the water falls dramatically and many animals die.

This whole process is known as **eutrophication**.

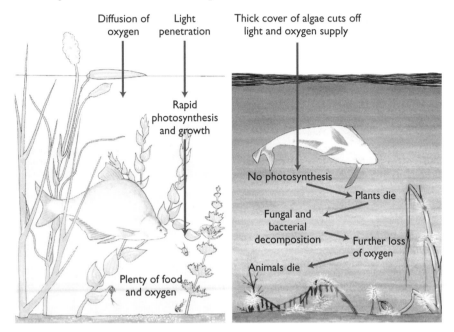

Figure 52 Effects of eutrophication

Eutrophication is *more* likely to occur in hot weather because:
- the mineral ions become more concentrated as a result of increased evaporation of water
- metabolic processes are speeded up due to increased enzyme activity

Eutrophication is *less* likely to occur in moving water than still water because:
- the mineral ions are rapidly diluted
- the water is being re-oxygenated continuously

What the examiners could ask you to do

- Explain any of the key concepts.
- Recall and show understanding of any of the key facts.
- Interpret data relating changes in atmospheric carbon dioxide concentration and the Earth's temperature.
- Interpret data relating global warming and the distribution of insects.
- Interpret data relating global warming and the yield of crop plants.
- Interpret data relating the use of fertilisers to crop yield and eutrophication.

Succession: how ecosystems change over time
Succession

Key concepts you must understand

Organisms that survive in an environment are adapted to that environment. If the environment changes, those organisms will be less well adapted to the changed environment. Other organisms may be better adapted and outcompete the original organisms, which may become locally extinct.

The ecosystems that exist today did not always exist. They have developed from other previous ecosystems by **succession**.

Succession often involves an initial colonisation of a hostile environment; the colonisers cause changes in the abiotic environment. These changes allow other species to enter the area because it is now less hostile. These species also modify the environment, causing further changes in the community. Therefore, the complexity of the food webs, which make up the community of the developing ecosystem, increases. The succession leads to a final, complex state called the **climax community**; when the succession reaches this stage, environmental factors prevent it developing further.

Key facts you must know and understand

An area with virtually no organisms may be colonised by a species with appropriate adaptations. As the population of this **pioneer species** grows, it interacts with the environment and changes it. The changes may allow other species to enter the area and cause further changes. A succession is illustrated in Figure 53.

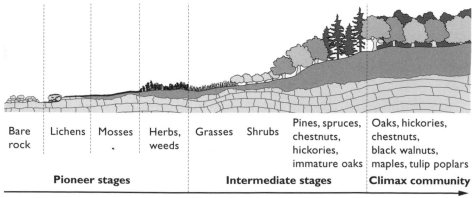

Bare rock	Lichens	Mosses	Herbs, weeds	Grasses	Shrubs	Pines, spruces, chestnuts, hickories, immature oaks	Oaks, hickories, chestnuts, black walnuts, maples, tulip poplars
Pioneer stages				**Intermediate stages**			**Climax community**

Hundreds of years →

Figure 53 A succession

In the example given:
- Lichens are the pioneer species that can grow on bare rock.
- The growth of the lichens on the rock fragments it and dead lichens add organic matter; a soil is beginning to form.
- Mosses start to grow in the soil and outcompete the lichens; the mosses add more organic matter to the soil, making it more fertile.
- This process of changing the environment and making it less hostile is repeated as grasses, shrubs and finally trees colonise the area.
- As more and bigger plants colonise the area, they offer more habitats and niches to animals and so the species richness increases.
- The mixed hardwoods (oak, hickory, chestnuts etc.) form the climax community; the ecosystem will not become any more complex.

As different types of vegetation enter the area, they affect the amount and depth of soil. This, in turn, allows other types of plant to enter. The increasing complexity of the plant community creates more and more ecological niches and so more animals will enter the area. The species diversity increases through the succession, until a climax is reached.

Forest in Europe does not become as complex as tropical rain forest because of the climate. Our mixed forests are said to be a **climatic climax** community.

Grassland in much of Europe would revert to woodland/forest if sheep and cattle did not graze it. They nip off the growing points at the tips of young tree shoots. Grasses grow from ground level and so can re-grow. These grasslands are a **grazing climax**.

Where a succession starts from bare, previously uncolonised, ground or from a newly formed pond with no life, the succession is a **primary succession**. Sometimes, communities are destroyed by fire. When a new succession begins in such an area it is a **secondary succession**.

Succession and conservation of ecosystems

Key concepts you must understand

Succession leads to change in an ecosystem, whereas conservation may require the ecosystem to be maintained in more or less the same condition.

People conserving ecosystems must interfere and manage the process of succession in such a way that the ecosystem does not change significantly.

Key facts you must know and understand

The management of heather moorland is used here as an example of managing succession. Heather moorland is often maintained as a habitat for grouse, but it also provides a habitat for other animals that would not exist elsewhere.

Heather plants are small woody shrubs. Where there is a dense cover of heather, it provides an ideal habitat for grouse. As the heather grows taller, the cover becomes less dense and the habitat is less suitable for grouse. There are four main stages in the life cycle of heather plants, described in the table below.

Phase	Duration/ years	Productivity and biomass of heather plants	Appearance of heather plants
Pioneer	0–6	Low biomass, high productivity	Small separate shrubs
Building	6–15	High biomass, high productivity	Individual plants intertwine to form a dense canopy
Mature	12–28	High biomass, decreasing productivity	Gaps begin to appear in the centre
Degenerate	20–30	High biomass, low productivity	Gaps increase and other plants begin to grow in the gaps

The degenerate phase is the start of a succession to mixed woodland as trees begin to grow in the gaps in the centre of heather plants.

This is prevented by burning the heather at approximately 20-year intervals. The fire is carefully managed so that it does not become too intense and damage the underground parts of the plants. These then regrow and the cycle starts again. Succession is prevented and the heather moor is conserved.

What the examiners could ask you to do

- Explain any of the key concepts.
- Recall and show understanding of any of the key facts.
- Interpret data on succession and conservation in terms of changing or maintaining habitats and niches.
- Interpret data on changing species diversity indices in terms of succession.

Inheritance: passing on genes from one generation to the next
Basic ideas

Key concepts you must understand

The chromosomes in most animal and plant cells (except the sex cells) exist in pairs called **homologous pairs**. The total number of chromosomes in such cells is the **diploid number** of chromosomes.

Because of **meiosis**, sex cells (**gametes**) have only one chromosome from each homologous pair. Sex cells have the **haploid** number of chromosomes (half the diploid number).

Genes controlling the same feature are present at the same place (**locus**) on the two homologous chromosomes. Put another way, each chromosome of a homologous pair carries genes for the same features in the same sequence. However, the **alleles** of the genes may be different. Alleles are different versions of the same gene.

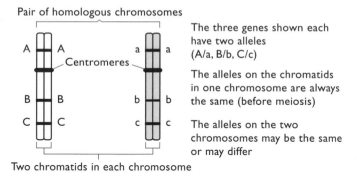

Figure 54 Homologous chromosomes

For example, in humans, the gene for phenylthiocarbamide (PTC) tasting has two alleles: one allele for being able to taste PTC and the other for not being able to taste PTC.

For any feature, the body cells contain two alleles that determine the feature. The alleles may be:

- the same (e.g. two alleles for tasting PTC); the organism is **homozygous** for the feature
- different (e.g. one allele for tasting PTC and one non-tasting allele); the organism is **heterozygous** for the feature

Alleles may be **dominant**, **recessive** or **codominant**. The different types of allele produce their effects under different circumstances, as shown in the table below.

Type of allele	Effect produced when homozygous?	Effect produced when heterozygous?
Dominant	Yes	Yes
Recessive	Yes	No
Codominant	Yes	Yes — both codominant alleles produce their effects

The **genotype** of an organism describes the genetic composition of that organism for a particular feature, or combination of features.

The **phenotype** of an organism is the feature resulting from the genotype.

The tables below illustrate the above ideas, using flower colour in plants as the examples.

Example 1: flower colour in pea plants

In the table, **P** represents the dominant allele for purple flower colour and **p** represents the recessive allele for white flower colour.

Genotype	Description of genotype	Phenotype	Reason for phenotype
PP	Homozygous for dominant allele (purple)	Purple flowers	Only the dominant allele (purple flowers) is present
Pp	Heterozygous	Purple flowers	The dominant allele (purple flowers) is always expressed in the heterozygote
pp	Homozygous for recessive allele (white)	White flowers	Only the recessive allele (white flowers) is present

Example 2: flower colour in snapdragons

In the table, C^R represents the codominant allele for red flower colour and C^W represents the codominant allele for white flower colour.

Genotype	Description of genotype	Phenotype	Reason for phenotype
$C^R C^R$	Homozygous for codominant red allele	Red flowers	Only the red codominant allele is present
$C^R C^W$	Heterozygous	Pink flowers	Both codominant alleles are present; both express themselves so red *and* white pigments are produced, resulting in pink flowers
$C^W C^W$	Homozygous for codominant white allele	White flowers	Only the white codominant allele is present

Some genes have more than two alleles — for example, ABO blood groups are controlled by three alleles. However, any one person only has two alleles for blood groups — one on each chromosome of a homologous pair.

The blood group of a person is determined by the presence or absence of two antigens (antigen A and antigen B) on the surface of the red blood cells. There are three alleles involved:

- I^A which determines the production of the A antigen.
- I^B which determines the production of the B antigen.
- I^O which determines that neither antigen is produced.

Alleles I^A and I^B are codominant; but I^O is recessive to both. The possible genotypes and phenotypes (blood groups) are shown in the table below.

Genotype	Phenotype (blood group)
$I^A I^A$, $I^A I^O$	A
$I^B I^B$, $I^B I^O$	B
$I^A I^B$	AB
$I^O I^O$	O

Some features are determined by genes carried on the sex chromosomes. These are called **sex-linked** features. Although a few of these are carried on the Y chromosome, most are carried on the X chromosome.

Key facts you must know and understand

- A **gene** is a section of DNA in a chromosome that determines a particular feature by coding for a particular protein. For example, in pea plants there is a gene for flower colour and in humans there is a gene for earlobe attachment.
- An **allele** is a particular form of a gene.
- An **antigen** is a protein on the plasma membrane of a cell.

Patterns of inheritance

Key concepts you must understand

Monohybrid inheritance

For any feature, in every cell, except the sex cells, there are two alleles of the gene that determines the feature. The sex cells are formed by meiosis and so, for any feature, have only one allele.

If an individual is homozygous, the two alleles in each cell are the same and all the individual's sex cells will have the same allele.

If the individual is heterozygous, the two alleles in each cell are different and 50% of the individual's sex cells will have one allele and 50% will have the other allele.

Fertilisation is a random event; any male sex cell could fertilise any female sex cell. There is an equal probability of all possible combinations of alleles occurring.

The study of the pattern of inheritance of a feature determined by a single pair of alleles is called **monohybrid inheritance**. Breeding pea plants over two generations and observing their flower colours allows us to see some of the patterns in monohybrid inheritance. The procedure is as follows:

- Obtain purple-flowered plants and white-flowered plants from pure breeding lines. Pure breeding purple-flowered plants produce only purple-flowered plants when they are self-pollinated.
- Cross-pollinate pure breeding (homozygous) purple-flowered plants with pure breeding (homozygous) white-flowered plants.
- Collect the seeds formed and germinate to give a new generation of pea plants — the **F1** generation.
- *Self*-pollinate the plants of the **F1** generation.
- Collect the seeds formed and germinate to give the **F2** generation.

The genetic diagram in Figure 55 summarises such a cross.

content guidance

Parental phenotype	Purple flowers	White flowers	Plants from pure-breeding lines are cross-pollinated
Parental genotype	PP	pp	Both are homozygous
Parental gametes	P	p	Gametes are haploid, so contain only one allele from a pair — only one type of gamete from each parent
F1 genotype		Pp	All F1 plants are heterozygous with purple flowers — purple allele is dominant
F1 gametes	P p	P p	All F1 plants can produce two types of gamete — half with the purple flower allele and half with the white flower allele (two sets are shown to represent male and female gametes)

F2 genotypes

	P	p
P	PP	Pp
p	Pp	PP

This is the standard way of showing all the possible fertilisations and possible combinations of alleles in the F2 generation

In this instance, three of the possible four combinations contain at least one dominant allele and so have purple flowers, while only one of the four has two recessive alleles to give white flowers

F2 phenotypes   3 purple flowers : 1 white flower

Figure 55 A cross between pure-breeding pea plants

Tip You may be asked to complete a genetic diagram such as that in Figure 55. Practise producing them and show all the stages. Often candidates leave out the 'gamete line' in genetic diagrams and then get confused in trying to work out possible combinations of alleles in the next generation. Learn to do it mechanically — it will then always produce the right answer.

The test cross

Pea plants with purple flowers can be either homozygous or heterozygous. To find out which is which, we must carry out a breeding experiment. We can predict possible outcomes if the purple-flowered plant is crossed with a plant of known genotype. So we cross it with a white-flowered plant, which, because the white allele is recessive, must have the genotype **pp**.

First, use a genetic diagram to make the predictions, as in Figure 56.

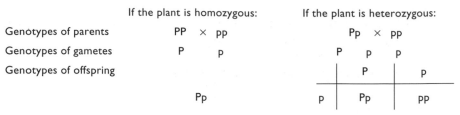

	If the plant is homozygous:		If the plant is heterozygous:		
Genotypes of parents	PP × pp		Pp × pp		
Genotypes of gametes	P p		P p	p	
Genotypes of offspring				P	p
			P	Pp	pp
	Pp		p		
Phenotypes of offspring	All have purple flowers		Half purple flowers, half white flowers		

Figure 56 A test cross

Carry out the cross, collect the seeds and germinate them. Any white-flowered plants that grow have inherited two recessive white alleles; one of these recessive alleles must have come from the purple-flowered parent. Therefore, the original purple-flowered plant was heterozygous.

If all the seeds produce purple-flowered plants, it is likely that the original plant was homozygous.

Tip Remember, if you are asked how you would discover if an organism is heterozygous or homozygous, you must breed it with one showing the recessive feature (carry out a test cross).

Working out which allele is dominant

If a pink male Kraken is crossed with a blue female Kraken and all the offspring are pink, there are two possibilities:

- Pink is dominant and, in each case, a dominant pink allele from the male combined with a recessive blue allele from the female.
- Blue is dominant and, in each case, a recessive pink allele from the male combined with a recessive pink from the female (who was heterozygous).

We simply do not know.

However, if two pink Krakens mated and there were some blue offspring, we can be certain that pink is dominant. How?

- The pink Krakens must have had pink alleles to be pink.
- They must have passed on blue alleles to produce blue offspring.
- The parent Krakens must have had both alleles.
- The parents were pink, so the pink allele must be dominant.

Tip The only way to know which allele is dominant is to look for two parents having the same feature (like the pink Krakens) having offspring with a different feature (the blue Krakens). The two parents must be heterozygous and the feature shown by the parents is the one determined by the dominant allele.

Pedigrees

A **pedigree** is a way of representing the inheritance of a feature over several generations in a particular 'family'. In a pedigree:

- each horizontal row represents a generation
- vertical lines link one generation to the preceding generation

Examples

The pedigrees below show:

- the pattern of inheritance of PTC tasting (if you can taste it, it is very bitter indeed), which is determined by a dominant allele, **T**
- the pattern of inheritance of albinism in a family, which is determined by a recessive allele, **n**

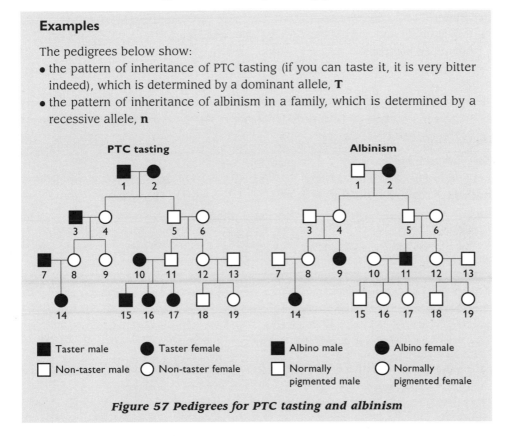

Figure 57 Pedigrees for PTC tasting and albinism

The key to accessing the information given in a pedigree is provided by those individuals showing the recessive feature. These individuals can only be homozygous and so:

- they must have inherited one recessive allele from each parent
- they will pass on one recessive allele to all their children

> **Tip** In an examination, you may be given a pedigree but not be told which feature is determined by the dominant allele. So, look for the situation we met earlier: do two parents with the same feature ever produce children with a different feature?

Look at the PTC pedigree example in Figure 57: individuals 1 and 2 can taste PTC, but their children cannot. Therefore:

- Individuals 1 and 2 must have the tasting alleles.

- They must have passed on non-tasting alleles to produce non-tasting offspring (individuals 4, 5 and 6).
- Individuals 1 and 2 must have both alleles and, because they were tasters, the tasting allele must be dominant.

If you had not been told which allele was dominant, similar logic could be used on the albinism pedigree:

- Individuals 3 and 4 must have normal pigmentation alleles to have normal (not albino) pigmentation.
- They must have passed on albinism alleles to produce albino offspring (individual 9).
- Individuals 3 and 4 must have both alleles and, because they had normal pigmentation, the normal pigmentation allele must be dominant and the allele for albinism must be recessive.

Sex-linked inheritance

Gender, in humans, is determined largely by the sex chromosomes: the genotype of males is **XY** and that of females is **XX**.

Genotypes of parents	XX		XY
Genotypes of gametes	X	X	Y
Genotypes of offspring		X	Y
	X	XX	XY

Phenotypes of offspring   1 female : 1 male

Figure 58 Determination of gender in humans

The X and Y chromosomes are largely non-homologous, so they carry different genes. Therefore:

- in males, a recessive allele on the single X chromosome will be expressed (as there can be no equivalent dominant allele on the Y chromosome)
- in females, a recessive allele must be present on both X chromosomes for it to be expressed

Males (XY) can only inherit alleles on the X chromosome from their mother. She can only pass on the X chromosome; the father passes on a Y chromosome to his sons.

Sex-linked features determined by recessive alleles on the X chromosome share the following characteristics:

- They are much more common among males (because females must inherit two X chromosomes carrying the recessive allele, whereas males must inherit only one).
- Affected males inherit the sex-linked allele from their mothers.
- Affected females inherit one allele from each parent (so the father will be affected).
- Females who are heterozygous for the condition are called carriers.

- They may 'skip' a generation and then appear *in the males only*.

Features determined by recessive alleles carried on the X chromosome include red–green colour blindness and haemophilia.

Genotypes of sex-linked features include the appropriate sex chromosomes as well as the alleles. For red–green colour blindness, **B** represents the allele for normal vision and **b** represents the allele for red–green colour blindness. The possible genotypes and phenotypes are:

- **X^{B}Y** — normal male
- **X^{b}Y** — affected male
- **X^{B}X^B** — normal female
- **X^{B}X^b** — carrier female (*not* colour blind)
- **X^{b}X^b** — affected female

Example

The pedigree shows the inheritance of red–green colour blindness in a family.

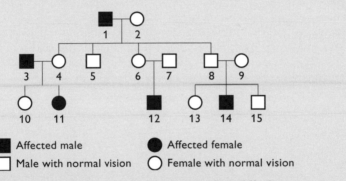

Figure 59 Inheritance of red–green colour blindness

If you were not told that this was a sex-linked feature, there are several hints:
- It clearly skips a generation.
- It is more common in the males.
- The only affected female has an affected father.

To work out the genotypes of individuals in a pedigree of a sex-linked feature, begin with a genotype of which you can be certain. This can be an affected male (e.g. genotype **X^{b}Y** — with the affected X chromosome inherited from his mother), an unaffected male (**X^{B}Y**) or an affected female (e.g. genotype **X^{b}X^b** — each parent has passed on one affected X chromosome).

You can now work backwards and forwards from this known starting point. In the example given in Figure 59, what are the genotypes of individuals 9 and 10?

- Individual 9 is the mother of individual 14 — an affected male ($X^b Y$). The X^b chromosome can only have come from the mother (individual 9) who is unaffected. She must therefore have the X^B chromosome and her genotype must be $X^B X^b$.
- Individual 10 is the daughter of individual 3 and is unaffected. She could be $X^B X^B$ (a normal female) or $X^B X^b$ (a carrier female). She inherits an X chromosome from each parent and so must inherit X^b from individual 3 (affected male). She must be $X^B X^b$ — a carrier female.

Tip When you are solving pedigrees like this, write on the pedigree diagram the genotypes of which you can be certain at the outset. This will help you to see where the various affected chromosomes have come from.

Inheritance involving codominance

Flower colour in snapdragons is determined by the codominant alleles C^R (red flowers) and C^W (white flowers). Possible genotypes and phenotypes are shown below:

- $C^R C^R$ — red flowers
- $C^W C^W$ — white flowers
- $C^R C^W$ — pink flowers

The heterozygote ($C^R C^W$) does not develop red or white flowers — it develops pink ones. This is because both alleles affect the colour of the flower.

In a cross between two heterozygotes, in which one allele shows complete dominance, the offspring ratio is 3:1 dominant to recessive. This is not the case with codominance.

Genotypes of parents	$C^R C^W$		$C^R C^W$	
Genotypes of gametes	C^R	C^W	C^R	C^W
Genotypes of offspring			C^R	C^W
	C^R		$C^R C^R$	$C^R C^W$
	C^W		$C^R C^W$	$C^W C^W$
Phenotypes of offspring			1 red : 2 pink : 1 white	

Figure 60 Flower colour in snapdragons is controlled by codominant alleles

The 3:1 ratio found in the cross between two heterozygotes showing complete dominance has been replaced by a 1:2:1 ratio.

This 1:2:1 ratio is also the ratio of the genotypes and is also found in the cross between heterozygotes with complete dominance.

Multiple-allele inheritance

In the inheritance of the ABO blood groups, the possible genotypes and phenotypes (blood groups) are shown in the table below.

Genotype	Phenotype (blood group)
I^AI^A, I^AI^O	A
I^BI^B, I^BI^O	B
I^AI^B	AB
I^OI^O	O

It is possible for parents to have four children, each with a different blood group. Remember, the I^A and I^B alleles are codominant and I^O is recessive to both.

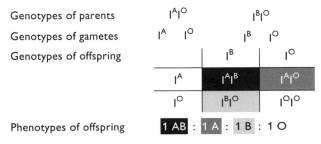

Phenotypes of offspring   1 AB : 1 A : 1 B : 1 O

Figure 61 Inheritance of blood groups

You may also be given pedigrees of features determined by multiple alleles. In such a case, you would be told that the feature was an example of this type of inheritance. Then the same principles hold true as for determining genotypes in other pedigrees — start from a known genotype and work forwards to children and back to parents. In the example below, there are two known genotypes: blood group AB can only have the genotype I^AI^B and blood group O can only have the genotype I^OI^O.

Worked example

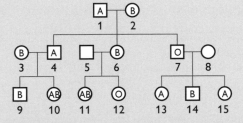

Figure 62 A blood-group pedigree

What are the blood groups of individuals 5 and 8?

Answer

Individual 5 must pass on an I^O allele to individual 12 who must have two (as she is blood group O). He must also pass on an I^A allele to individual 11, who is blood group AB and cannot have inherited this from her mother, who is blood group B).

Individual 5 therefore has the genotype I^AI^O and is blood group A.

Individual 8 must be blood group AB. Individual 7 is blood group O (genotype I^OI^O) and so can only pass on I^O alleles. The I^A and I^B alleles in children 13 and 14 *must* therefore have come from individual 8.

Genes in populations

Key concepts you must understand

Basic ideas

A population is a group of individuals of a particular species found in a habitat at any given time.

The **gene pool** is all the genes and all their alleles that are present in a population.

Populations with a large gene pool have high genetic diversity. Such populations can withstand changes in the environment, as some individuals will have the necessary adaptations to survive.

Populations with a small gene pool have low genetic diversity. Such populations are more likely to become extinct as a result of changes in the environment.

Within a gene pool, every allele or gene variant has a particular **frequency**.

The frequency of an allele is the number of occurrences of that allele in that population as a proportion of the number of occurrences of all the alleles of that gene. It is usually expressed as a decimal fraction, e.g. 0.6.

The sum of the frequencies of all the alleles of a gene must, therefore, equal 1.

Example

Consider a population of 15 Krakens, some pink and some blue. Skin colour is controlled by a single gene with two alleles: **P** (pink) is dominant and **p** (blue) is recessive.

- There are 15 individual Krakens in the population, so there are 30 alleles of the coat colour gene.
- Six alleles in this population are **P** (pink) and 24 are **p** (blue).

The frequencies of these alleles are:

- 24/30 of the genes in the gene pool are **b** — a frequency of **0.8**
- 6/30 of the genes in the gene pool are **B** — a frequency of **0.2**

The Hardy–Weinberg equation

The Hardy–Weinberg equation allows us to estimate the frequency of an allele in a population. To do so, however, certain conditions must be met. These include:

- There is a large population.
- Individual organisms are diploid.
- The individuals reproduce sexually and mating is random.
- Mutation does not occur.
- There is no natural selection.
- There is no migration.

In practice, only the first two of these conditions can be met in full. Others are not met — for example, in animals, there will be some kind of sexual selection, so mating is not random.

Example: modelling allele frequencies

Suppose that a gene has two alleles **A** and **a** and that there are equal numbers of each allele in the population.

We can model the situation by representing these alleles using red balls (**A**) and black balls (**a**).
- Place 25 red (**A**) and 25 black (**a**) balls into each of two bags — the bags represent the males and females in the population.
- Withdraw one ball at random from each bag and note the colours you have withdrawn — this represents a 'random mating'.
- Replace the balls.
- Repeat until you have results for 100 'random matings'.
- Calculate the frequencies of the three possible genotypes (**AA**, **Aa** and **aa**).

What percentages could we predict?
- On every occasion, there is an equal chance of drawing **A** or **a**.
- Therefore, from 100 attempts, we would expect to draw 50 **A** and 50 **a** from the male and 50 **A** and 50 **a** from the female.
- The table below shows the likely combinations of alleles.

	50 **A**	50 **a**
50 **A**	25 **AA**	25 **Aa**
50 **a**	25 **Aa**	25 **aa**

- We would predict 25% **AA** : 50% **Aa** : 25% **aa**.
- This is the 1:2:1 ratio of genotypes obtained from crossing two heterozygotes.

The Hardy–Weinberg equations assume that the frequency of an allele is the same in males and females.

In these equations for a gene with two alleles:

- The frequency of the dominant allele is represented by p.
- The frequency of the recessive allele is represented by q.
- There are no other alleles of this particular gene, so:
  $p + q = 1$ This is the first Hardy–Weinberg equation.
- The frequency of the dominant homozygote (**AA** in the example above) is
  p (male) $\times p$ (female) $= p^2$.
- The frequency of the recessive homozygote (**aa** in the example above) is
  q (male) $\times q$ (female) $= q^2$.
- The frequency of the heterozygote (**Aa** in the example above) is
  (p (male) $\times q$ (female)) + (p (female) $\times q$ (male)) $= 2pq$.
- This accounts for all the possible genotypes, so:
  $p^2 + 2pq + q^2 = 1$ This is the second Hardy–Weinberg equation.

If you know any of the values p, q, p^2 or q^2, you can calculate all the others.

Worked example 1

A dominant allele, **A**, has a frequency of 0.6 in a population. Calculate the frequency of the heterozygotes in the population.

Answer

$p = 0.6$

because $p + q = 1$ (first Hardy–Weinberg equation)

$q = (1 - 0.6) = 0.4$

The frequency of the heterozygote is $2pq$

$2pq = 2 \times 0.6 \times 0.4 = 0.48$

The frequency of the heterozygotes is 0.48.

Worked example 2

In a population, 64% of people can taste PTC. PTC tasting is determined by a dominant allele. Calculate the frequency of the dominant allele.

Answer

The PTC tasters include the dominant homozygotes and the heterozygotes. In the second Hardy–Weinberg equation, this is represented by $p^2 + 2pq$

So, remainder of the population are recessive homozygotes $= q^2$

Remainder of the population = 100% (the whole population) – 64% (the dominant homozygotes and the heterozygotes) = 36% or 0.36

$q^2 = 0.36$

$q = \sqrt{0.36} = 0.6$

but, because $p + q = 1$

p (frequency of dominant allele) = $(1.0 - 0.6) = 0.4$

If we know the size of the population, we can then work out actual *numbers* of each genotype:

number in population × frequency of genotype

For example, in the above example, if the population size was 450, then the number of individuals showing the recessive genotype is:

0.36 (q^2) × 450 = 162

Tip In calculations involving the Hardy–Weinberg equation, you must carry out the calculations using decimals. If you are given information about frequencies in percentages, change them to a decimal fraction (divide the percentage by 100) before you use it — for example, 64% = 64 ÷ 100 = 0.64.

What the examiners could ask you to do:

- Explain any of the key concepts.
- Recall and show understanding of any of the key facts.
- From genetic crosses, pedigrees and other information:
  - deduce, giving reasons, whether a feature is determined by a dominant or recessive allele, whether it exhibits codominance and whether it is sex-linked
  - deduce, giving reasons, genotypes and/or phenotypes of specified individuals
  - predict the likely offspring from specified crosses
- Use your knowledge of meiosis from AS (Unit 2) to explain why sex cells only carry single copies of a gene
- Use the Hardy–Weinberg equations to calculate, from data supplied:
  - allele frequencies
  - genotype frequencies
  - numbers of individuals with a particular allele or genotype

Selection and speciation: the origin of new species
Selection

Key concepts you must understand

In his theory of natural selection, Charles Darwin proposed that: 'Those members of a species which are best adapted to their environment will survive and reproduce in greater numbers than others less well adapted.'

The features that give organisms an advantage are determined by alleles. The following will happen:

- The individuals with the advantageous allele will survive to reproduce in greater numbers than those without the advantageous allele.
- They will pass on the advantageous allele in greater numbers than other organisms pass on the less favourable allele for the same gene.
- The advantageous allele will increase in frequency in the next generation.
- This will repeat over many generations, until most of the population possess the advantageous allele.

> **Tip** Do not fall into the trap of assuming that because an allele is dominant, it must be advantageous — the two are not linked.

Suppose that a feature is controlled by two alleles **A** and **a**. Initially, neither allele gives more advantage than the other and each allele has a frequency of 0.5. The environment changes and allele **a** gives a selective advantage to the organism, but allele **A** does not. The frequencies of the two alleles will change over time:

- The frequency of allele **a** will increase.
- The frequency of allele **A** will decrease (see Figure 63).

Directional selection

Some features show a range of values, rather than just the 'either/or' condition we have considered so far. The numbers of individuals at each point on the range reflect the survival value to the population of that particular value. The mean value represents the value that is best adapted to a particular environment.

If the environment changes, individuals at one extreme may have an advantage while those at the other extreme have a disadvantage. Over time, selection operates against the disadvantaged extreme and in favour of the other extreme. The mean and range of values shift towards the favoured extreme (see Figure 64).

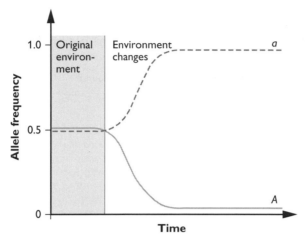

Figure 63 Change in allele frequency over time

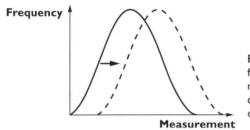

Environmental changes favour the selection of more suitable phenotypes, causing the normal distribution to shift

Figure 64 Directional selection

Example

Peccaries feed on cacti. They eat those that have fewest spines. So, when peccaries enter an area where cacti are growing, they exert a 'selection pressure' on the cacti. Those with the most spines have an advantage; those with fewest spines are at a selective disadvantage. Those with the most spines survive and reproduce more effectively than those with fewer spines. Over time, the mean number of spines per cactus increases in the population.

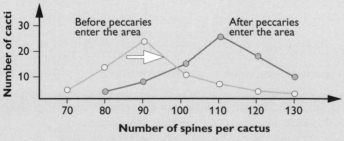

Figure 65 Directional selection in cacti

Stabilising selection

In a stable environment, selection operates against *both extremes* of a range. It operates to maintain the 'status quo' in the population and to make the population more uniform.

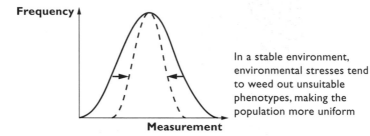

In a stable environment, environmental stresses tend to weed out unsuitable phenotypes, making the population more uniform

Figure 66 Stabilising selection

Birth mass in humans is an example. Babies who are very heavy or very light show a higher neonatal mortality rate (die more frequently at or just after birth) than those of medium mass. Over time, selection operates to reduce the numbers of heavy and light babies born.

Speciation

Key concepts you must understand

Natural selection explains how populations of a species become adapted to their environment and change in a changing environment. But how does a new species arise?

A key part of the definition of a species is 'a group of interbreeding organisms that produce viable and fertile offspring'. If two groups cannot interbreed to produce fertile and viable offspring, they must be different species.

As long as two populations are able to interbreed, they are unlikely to evolve into distinct species. They must somehow undergo a period of isolation — a period where they are prevented from interbreeding. During this period, mutations that occur in one population are not transferred to the other; so genetic differences between the populations can increase. These differences can become so great that, after some time, the populations are reproductively isolated, i.e. they cannot interbreed and are now distinct species.

There are several ways in which populations can be reproductively isolated.

Geographical isolation occurs when the two populations are physically separated. Interbreeding is impossible and speciation may result. Speciation as a result of geographical isolation is called **allopatric speciation**.

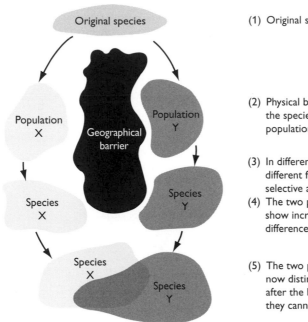

(1) Original species

(2) Physical barrier divides the species into two populations

(3) In different environments, different features have a selective advantage

(4) The two populations show increasing genetic differences

(5) The two populations are now distinct species; even after the barrier has gone they cannot interbreed

Figure 67 Allopatric speciation

Other types of isolation need not involve physical separation. The two diverging populations may inhabit the same area, but be prevented from interbreeding in one of the following ways:

- Seasonal isolation — members of the two populations reproduce at different times of the year.
- Temporal isolation — members of the two populations reproduce at different times of the day.
- Behavioural isolation — members of the two populations have different courtship patterns.

Speciation following any of these methods of isolation is called **sympatric speciation**.

What the examiners could ask you to do

- Explain any of the key concepts.
- Recall and show understanding of any of the key facts.
- Identify, from data supplied, how selection is acting in a given situation and explain the likely results of selection on genotypes, phenotypes and allele frequencies.
- Deduce, from graphs and other data, whether selection is directional or stabilising.
- Deduce from information supplied whether speciation is taking place in a given situation and whether the process is allopatric or sympatric.

Questions
&
Answers

This section contains questions similar in style to those you can expect to see in your Unit 4 examination. The limited number of questions in this guide means that it is impossible to cover all the topics and all the question styles, but they should give you a flavour of what to expect. The responses that are shown are real students' answers to the questions.

There are several ways of using this section. You could:

- 'hide' the answers to each question and try the question yourself. It needn't be a memory test — use your notes to see if you can actually make all the points you ought to make
- check your answers against the candidates' responses and make an estimate of the likely standard of your response to each question
- check your answers against the examiner's comments to see where you might have lost marks
- check your answers against the terms used in the question — did you *explain* when you were asked to, or did you merely *describe*?

Examiner's comments

All candidate responses are followed by examiner's comments. These are preceded by the icon ⎋ and indicate where credit is due. In the weaker answers, they also point out areas for improvement, specific problems and common errors such as lack of clarity, weak or non-existent development, irrelevance, misinterpretation of the question and mistaken meanings of terms.

Food chains and food webs

The diagram shows a food web in decaying plant matter.

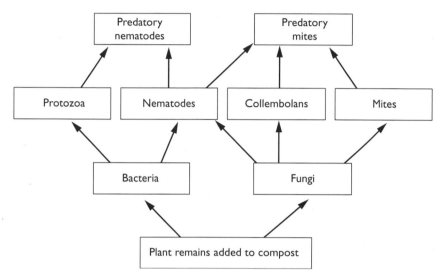

(a) For the food chain:

plant remains → bacteria → nematodes → predatory nematodes

construct:
(i)   a pyramid of numbers   (1 mark)
(ii) a pyramid of biomass   (1 mark)

(b) A disease reduces the numbers of predatory nematodes. This could lead
to a decrease in the breakdown of plant remains added to the compost.
Explain how.   (3 marks)

Total: 5 marks

■ ■ ■

Candidates' answers to Question 1

Candidate A
(a) (i)

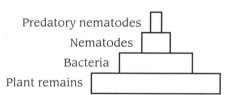

Candidate B

(a) (i)

Predatory mites ☐ Predatory nematodes

Protozoa, nematodes ☐ Mites

Bacteria and fungi ☐

Plant remains

🖉 Candidate A does not appreciate that bacteria are much smaller than any plant, and so there must be more of them. Candidate B has drawn an appropriate pyramid of numbers, but has labelled it incorrectly. Neither candidate scores a mark. If asked to interpret unusual food webs like this, make sure that you understand the principles of constructing ecological pyramids — and think about the size of organisms. Be careful not to lose marks through silly slips when you understand the biology.

Candidate A	**Candidate B**
(a) (ii)	**(a) (ii)**

Predatory nematodes ☐   Predatory nematodes ☐

Nematodes ☐   Nematodes ☐

Bacteria ☐   Bacteria ☐

Plant remains ☐   Plant remains ☐

🖉 Both candidates have drawn the pyramid correctly.

Candidate A

(b) The bacteria and fungi won't break down the plant remains as fast.

Candidate B

(b) Because there are fewer predatory nematodes, the numbers of protozoa and ordinary nematodes will increase, because there is less predation. This means that they will consume more bacteria and the nematodes will consume more fungi as well. So there will be fewer bacteria and fungi breaking down the plant remains.

🖉 Candidate B understands the relationships between the trophic levels and gives a full account of the changes. Candidate B scores all 3 marks. Candidate A hasn't explained why there will be less breakdown and fails to score.

🖉 **Both candidates should have been able to score full marks on part (a). Part (b) is not particularly difficult and an average candidate should score a couple of marks here. Overall, Candidate A scores 1 mark and Candidate B scores 4 marks.**

Hardy–Weinberg

King cheetahs have a different pattern of spots from ordinary cheetahs. The king cheetah coat pattern is the result of a mutation. The resulting allele is recessive to that for normal coat pattern. A population of 100 cheetahs contained nine king cheetahs.

(a) At first, it was thought that the two might be different species. How could it have been proved that they were members of the same species? (2 marks)

(b) Use the Hardy–Weinberg equation to calculate:
  (i)   the *frequency* of the dominant allele (2 marks)
  (ii) the *number* of heterozygotes in the population (2 marks)

(c) Give *two* reasons why the use of the Hardy–Weinberg equation might not be valid on this occasion. (2 marks)

Total: 8 marks

■ ■ ■

Candidates' answers to Question 2

Candidate A

(a) They could breed them and see if they produced offspring.

Candidate B

(a) If a king cheetah and a normal cheetah are bred together and they produce offspring that can also have offspring, then they must be the same species.

  ℮ Candidate B gives a more complete answer than Candidate A. Candidate A scores 1 mark; Candidate B scores 2 marks.

Candidate A

(b) (i) There are 9 in 100 king cheetahs so this is 9% dominant alleles.

Candidate B

(b) (i) There are 9 in 100 = 9% king cheetahs. They have double recessive alleles so in Hardy–Weinberg this is q^2. So $q^2 = 9\%$ or 0.09
So $q = 0.3$ and $p = 0.7$

Candidate A

(b) (ii) There are 91 ordinary cheetahs and probably two-thirds of these are heterozygous. This is 60.66 cheetahs.

Candidate B

(b) (ii) Heterozygotes = $2pq = 2 \times 0.3 \times 0.7 = 0.42$

so numbers of heterozygotes = $0.42 \times 100 = 42$

Candidate A does not understand the Hardy–Weinberg principle and fails to score. Candidate B demonstrates that, once you do, it is easy to score full marks on this type of calculation. Candidate B scores all 4 marks for part (b).

Candidate A

(c) The Hardy–Weinberg equations are only valid when there is a large population and 100 isn't that many. The king cheetah is a mutation and they aren't supposed to happen in Hardy–Weinberg.

Candidate B

(c) The Hardy–Weinberg equations are only valid for large populations and where there is no mutation.

 Both candidates understand the limitations of Hardy–Weinberg, although Candidate B expresses this better. However, there is an important point here. Although Candidate A's expression is clumsy, the ideas are correct. Don't be put off if you don't know the exact words; you could still score full marks. Both candidates score 2 marks.

 Candidate A scores 3 marks, Candidate B scores 8. This is a question where understanding of concepts is important.

Question 3

Aerobic respiration

The diagram shows some of the stages in respiration.

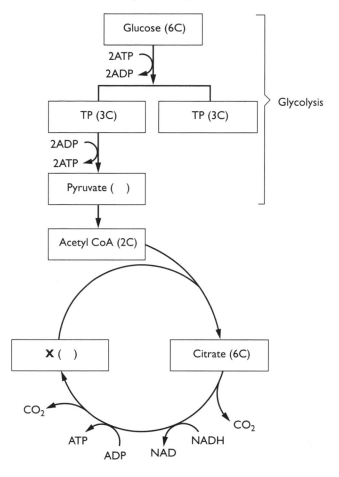

(a) (i) How many carbon atoms are present in pyruvate and in
compound **X**? *(1 mark)*

(ii) How many **ATP** molecules are generated during glycolysis?
Explain your answer. *(2 marks)*

(b) What becomes of the reduced **NAD** generated in glycolysis and
the Krebs cycle? *(2 marks)*

Total: 5 marks

Candidates' answers to Question 3

Candidate A

(a) (i) Pyruvate has three carbon atoms and compound X has four.

Candidate B

(a) (i) Pyruvate is a 3C compound whereas compound X is a 4C compound.

> Both candidates are awarded the mark.

Candidate A

(a) (ii) No ATPs are generated during glycolysis. Actually, two are generated but two are used up as well.

Candidate B

(a) (ii) There is a net profit of two ATP molecules during glycolysis. Two are used when glucose is converted to fructose 1,6-bisphosphate, but later four molecules are generated by substrate-level phosphorylation.

> Candidate A does not appreciate that each molecule of glucose produces two molecules of ATP and so, from this point on, all ATP yields per molecule must be doubled. However, the candidate has spotted that there is energy investment, as well as energy yield, and so 1 mark is awarded. Candidate B gives an excellent answer for 2 marks — but it does go well beyond the requirements.

Candidate A

(b) The reduced NAD is used in the electron transport chain.

Candidate B

(b) The reduced NAD (NADH) is re-oxidised to NAD in the electron transfer system. It loses hydrogen ions and electrons. The electrons lose energy along the electron transfer system to generate ATP. The NAD formed can be used again in glycolysis and the Krebs cycle.

> Candidate A knows that the electron transport chain is involved, for 1 mark, but has missed the key point that the NAD is re-oxidised. Candidate B has, again, gone well beyond what is required. The question asks 'What becomes of the *reduced NAD?*'. It does not ask for details of what becomes of the *electrons*. However, Candidate B does make both key points about the fate of the reduced NAD — it is re-oxidised in the electron transport chain. *Read the question carefully and try not to supply too much detail.*

> **This is a fairly typical question on respiration and a grade-C candidate ought to be able to score well. Candidate A scores 3 marks and Candidate B scores full marks.**

Greenhouse effect

The diagram shows the energy exchanges between the **Sun, Earth** and space in a situation where the average temperature of the Earth is stable at **14°C**. (Figures for energy exchange are watts per square metre of the Earth's surface.)

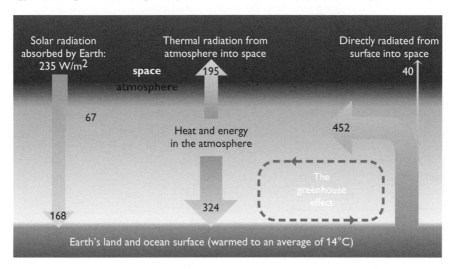

(a) **Name** *two* greenhouse gases. (2 marks)

(b) **Use figures from the diagram to explain why the surface of the Earth stays at a constant 14°C.** (4 marks)

(c) **Use figures from the diagram to explain what would happen to the temperature of the Earth if there were no greenhouse effect.** (4 marks)

Total: 10 marks

Candidates' answers to Question 4

Candidate A
(a) Carbon dioxide and ozone are greenhouse gases.

Candidate B
(a) Carbon dioxide and methane

> ✐ The inclusion of ozone shows that Candidate A is confusing the greenhouse effect with a different aspect of atmospheric pollution. The candidate scores just 1 mark, for carbon dioxide. Candidate B scores both marks.

Candidate A
(b) It stays the same temperature because it is losing as much heat as it gains.

Candidate B

(b) Total energy absorbed by the Earth's surface is $168 + 324 = 492$. To stay the same temperature, it must lose the same amount of heat.

> 🖉 Candidate A understands that for the temperature to remain constant, heat loss and heat gain must balance, but has not made any attempt at explanation. The question states *'use figures from the diagram to explain why…'*. If you don't use the figures in such a question, you cannot score full marks. Candidate B begins to use the figures, but does not explain how the figures are balanced. The 492 W m^{-2} that are gained are balanced by 452 W m^{-2} lost to the atmosphere and 40 W m^{-2} radiated directly into space. Candidate A scores 1 mark; Candidate B scores 3 marks.

Candidate A

(c) If there was no greenhouse effect then global warming wouldn't take place. The planet would be cooler and the ice caps wouldn't be melting.

Candidate B

(c) The Earth's temperature would be lower if there was no global warming. It's the greenhouse effect that keeps the planet habitable. But too much greenhouse effect is causing global warming and melting the ice caps. This means that the oceans will rise and some lands will be flooded. If all the energy reflected back to Earth by the greenhouse effect was lost to space, the Earth would cool down rapidly. 452 W m^{-2} is lost in the diagram.

> 🖉 Candidate A once again makes no use of the figures and scores just 1 mark for understanding the principle. Candidate B commits a serious offence in examinations — he/she strays off the point into a related area, but one that will score no marks. Candidate B must have spent a couple of minutes thinking about, and writing the description of, the consequences of the greenhouse effect, but this is not required by this question. Make sure that you *stick to the point*. Right at the end of the answer, Candidate B makes a superficial use of the figures and scores 1 mark.

> 🖉 **Candidate A scores 3 marks; Candidate B scores 6. Reading the questions carefully is always important, but particularly so here. The instruction in parts (b) and (c) to 'use the figures' means that there is a huge penalty if you do not.**

Nitrogen cycle

The diagram represents the circulation of nitrogen in an aquarium.
High concentrations of nitrates are toxic to many animals.

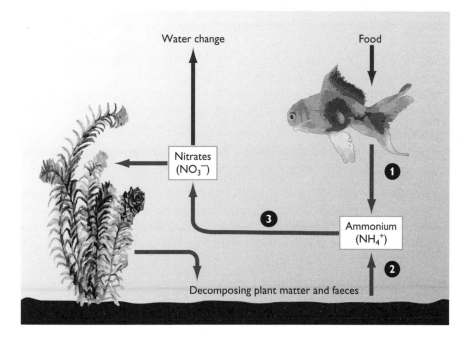

(a) Name the process labelled 1. (1 mark)

(b) Describe how ammonium ions are formed in the process labelled 2. (3 marks)

(c) Name the process labelled 3 and explain why it can be described as oxidation. (2 marks)

(d) Explain why the water in the aquarium should be changed regularly. (2 marks)

Total: 8 marks

■ ■ ■

Candidates' answers to Question 5

Candidate A
(a) Excretion

Candidate B
(a) Decay

> ✍ Both answers are valid. Fish do excrete ammonia, which would become ammonium ions in water. Dead fish would decay and ammonia would be released from the nitrogen-containing compounds. Both candidates score the mark.

Candidate A

(b) The dead remains are decomposed.

Candidate B

(b) Decomposers decay the dead remains. The ammonium comes from proteins in the remains.

> Neither candidate gives a complete description of the process. Both identify it correctly and score 1 mark for this. Candidate B identifies the source of the ammonium and so just scores a second mark.

Candidate A

(c) Process 3 is denitrification. It's an oxidation process because it uses oxygen.

Candidate B

(c) Process 3 is nitrification. It can be described as an oxidation process because the ammonium loses its hydrogen and replaces it with oxygen.

> Candidate A does not know the name of the stage and scores 1 mark for describing oxidation. Candidate B has the correct name and gives a better description of how the oxygen is used, for 2 marks.

Candidate A

(d) If it wasn't changed the ammonium will build up and it would poison the fish.

Candidate B

(d) If the water isn't changed, nitrification will use up all the oxygen in the water and the fish will die from asphyxiation.

> Candidate A scores 2 marks for an accurate description. Candidate B has a reasonable idea, but oxygen would be replaced from the atmosphere, so Candidate B fails to score.

> **Both candidates score 5 marks. Many candidates confuse the names of processes in the nitrogen cycle, yet there aren't that many to remember. There is no short cut — you just have to learn them. This is a relatively straightforward question and well-prepared candidates who had read the question carefully and looked carefully at the diagram would score higher marks.**

Question 6

Inheritance

Andalusian fowl can have plumage that have three distinct colours:

- black
- white
- blue

In breeding experiments, the following results were obtained:

Parents	black × white
Offspring	all blue

Parents	blue × blue
Offspring	white : black : blue
	1 : 2 : 1

(a) **Suggest an explanation for these results. Use evidence from the crosses to support your explanation.** (4 marks)

(b) **If a blue fowl were bred with a white fowl, what offspring would you expect? Explain your answer.** (4 marks)

Total: 8 marks

■ ■ ■

Candidates' answers to Question 6

Candidate A
(a) It looks like incomplete dominance. Blue is a new colour produced by parents who are black and white. If the black parent had two genes for black and the white parent had two genes for white, the children could have one gene for black and one gene for white, which would produce blue.

Candidate B
(a) If the parents are homozygous for black and white, they could have blue offspring if black and white were codominant.

P $\quad C^B C^B \quad \times \quad C^W C^W$
G $\quad C^B \quad\quad\quad C^W$
$F_1 \quad\quad C^B C^W$

Two blue parents could produce a mixture of offspring:

P $\quad C^B C^W \quad \times \quad C^B C^W$
G $\quad C^B \; C^W \quad C^B \; C^W$
$F_1 \quad C^B C^B \quad C^B C^W \quad C^B C^W \quad C^W C^W$

📝 Candidate A clearly understands the concept of codominance (although he/she uses the older name of incomplete dominance) and explains the first cross effectively. However, there is no explanation of the second cross and he/she uses the term gene where the term allele should be used. Even so, Candidate A scores 3 marks. Candidate B sets out the explanation more clearly but doesn't offer a key to explain the symbols and doesn't relate the genotypes to phenotypes. Candidate B also scores 3 marks.

Candidate A

(b) If you bred blue and white together, you would probably get the same again. You couldn't get black offspring because that would need two genes for black.

Candidate B

(b) P $\quad C^B C^W \quad \times \quad C^W C^W$

G $\quad C^B \quad C^W \quad C^W \quad C^W$

F_1 $\quad C^B C^W \quad C^W C^W \quad C^B C^W \quad C^W C^W$

There would be equal numbers of blue and white offspring.

📝 Candidate A scores 2 marks for describing the correct result and for giving a partial explanation. Candidate B has once more tried to use the correct format for a genetic diagram, but has not explained the symbols and has not linked genotypes to phenotypes. Both candidates score 2 marks.

📝 **Both candidates score 5 marks. Candidate B has a better approach, although Candidate A could have scored full marks with a more complete explanation. If you draw a genetic diagram, you *must*:**
- **explain the symbols you use**
- **state the phenotype that will result from each genotype in the offspring**

Q7 Question

Energy and food production

Organisms that reduce the yield of a crop plant are called pests. They can be controlled using pesticides, by biological control or by integrated crop management.

The figure shows the effects of repeated pesticide applications on a population of pests.

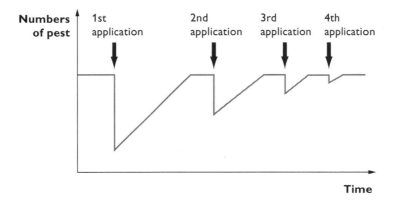

(a) (i) Suggest two reasons why the first application of the pesticide does not reduce the pest population to zero. (2 marks)

(ii) Explain the reduction in effect of the pesticide at the second, third and fourth applications. (3 marks)

(b) Give one benefit of each of the following in an integrated crop management system:

(i) crop rotation (not growing the same crop in the same field in successive years)

(ii) using organic fertilisers (such as farmyard manure) rather than inorganic fertilisers

(iii) planting crops that are tolerant of the local soil pH conditions (3 marks)

Total: 8 marks

■ ■ ■

Candidates' answers to Question 7

Candidate A

(a) (i) The dose might not have been strong enough and some of them might not have been affected by it.

Candidate B

(a) (i) Some of the pests might have a mutation that gives them resistance to the pesticide. Insecticides are usually sprayed and not all the pests are 'hit'.

What does Candidate A mean by 'not strong enough' and 'not affected by it'? Probably that the concentration of the insecticide wasn't strong enough to be toxic in some cases and that some of the pests were resistant. But this is not what the examiner is reading. Candidate A scores 1 mark — 'not strong enough' is too vague, but 'may not be affected by it' does seem to convey the idea of resistance. This is *my* opinion — another examiner might decide that both are too vague and award no marks. Candidate B makes two valid points and is awarded 2 marks. Learn, and try to use, the appropriate biological terms.

Candidate A

(a) (ii) More of the pests become immune to the pesticide. These survive and those that aren't immune are killed and so there are less of them.

Candidate B

(a) (ii) Some of the pests are resistant and these survive the initial application. These reproduce so that when the insecticide is re-applied, fewer of the pests are killed.

Neither candidate has offered a full explanation, although both seem to understand the ideas. Candidate A talks about immunity, which is wrong — you become immune to antigens, not pesticides. There is a hint, however, that as time goes by, there will be more of the resistant forms in the population and less of the non-resistant forms. Candidate A scores just 1 mark. Candidate B makes two points clearly — the difference in survival between resistant and non-resistant forms and that this will lead to more resistant forms reproducing compared with non-resistant forms. This is repeated with each application (a point which neither makes) and, each time, the proportion of resistant forms in the population increases. Candidate B scores 2 marks.

Candidate A

(b) (i) Insect pests won't have the same crops to feed on and so they die out.

Candidate B

(b) (i) The pests probably feed mainly on one crop plant, so by changing the crop every year you don't get a build up of any one pest. It might not kill them off though.

Both candidates appear to understand the effects of crop rotation. Each scores 1 mark.

Candidate A

(b) (ii) To supply what the plant needs in a natural form.

Candidate B

(b) (ii) Organic fertilisers don't supply all the minerals all at once; they release them slowly, like a 'drip-feed'.

Candidate A's answer is a good example of the sort of thing you should *never* write. It conveys about as much biological information as saying vegetables have a lot of 'goodness' in them. Be precise and be accurate. Candidate B has the right idea, for 1 mark.

Candidate A

(b) (iii) If they weren't from the area, and the soil was too acid, they might not grow properly.

Candidate B

(b) (iii) They will be able to compete effectively with any local weeds, which will also be adapted to the conditions.

Both candidates understand the benefit and are awarded 1 mark.

Much of this question is straightforward and examiners would expect a grade-C candidate to score 4 or 5 of the 7 marks available. A grade-A candidate should do better. The hardest part of this question is part (a) (ii), where clear explanation is required. Make sure that you write clearly in such situations. If you find it easier to write a series of bullet-pointed statements as an explanation, then do so. Candidate A scores 4 marks; Candidate B scores 7.

Selection and speciation

The graph shows the distribution of root length in a population of a species of grass. The population inhabits an area in which the soil water is held mainly in the top 20 cm.

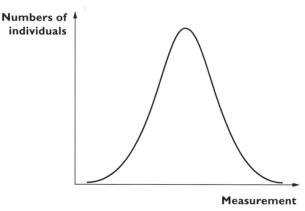

(a) What does the term 'population' mean? (1 mark)

(b) (i) Sketch, on the graph, the distribution of root lengths you would expect if some of these plants now colonised a different area where the soil water was held mainly below 20 cm. (1 mark)

(ii) Name, with a reason, the type of selection operating in this example. (1 mark)

(iii) Describe the evolutionary mechanisms that would lead to this change in the distribution of root lengths. (4 marks)

(c) In time, these populations may evolve into different species.

(i) Would this be an example of sympatric or allopatric speciation? Explain your answer. (1 mark)

(ii) Describe and explain the conditions essential for speciation to occur. (2 marks)

Total: 10 marks

■ ■ ■

Candidates' answers to Question 8

Candidate A

(a) A group of individuals living in the same place at the same time.

Candidate B

(a) A population is a group of the same species living in the same place.

    ✎ Only Candidate B gains the mark as the key ideas of same species and same place are included. Candidate A does not make clear that the individuals are of the same species.

Candidate A
(b) (i)

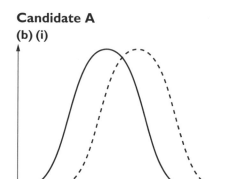

Candidate B
(b) (i)

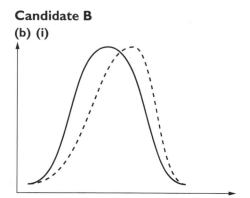

e Only Candidate A is awarded the mark as this graph shows the whole distribution shifting towards the longer-rooted extreme.

Candidate A

(b) (ii) Directional selection, because one extreme has an advantage over the other.

Candidate B

(b) (ii) Directional selection, because selection favours the longer-rooted plants as they can obtain the deep water more easily.

e Both candidates score the mark, but Candidate B has phrased the answer better.

Candidate A

(b) (iii) Those with the longer roots can survive better and breed because they can reach the water. The short-rooted plants die out by natural selection.

Candidate B

(b) (iii) The longer-rooted plants have a selective advantage because their roots can obtain water more efficiently than those with short roots. So the long-rooted plants survive and reproduce and pass on their 'long root' genes to their offspring. This keeps happening each generation so there are more and more long-rooted plants as time goes by.

e Both candidates appreciate the idea of selective advantage and Candidate B understands the mechanisms of natural selection. However, neither candidate explains how the whole distribution shifts to the right on the graph. There are some plants with even longer roots than before. This can be explained either by new combinations of genes or by gene mutation — or a combination of the two. Candidate A scores 2 marks and Candidate B scores 3 marks.

Candidate A

(c) (i) Allopatric speciation

Candidate B

(c) (i) Allopatric speciation because they do not interbreed.

e Both candidates choose the correct term, but neither scores a mark. Candidate A gives no reason and the reason given by Candidate B is insufficient. It does not make clear that they do not interbreed because they are geographically isolated. *You must know and be able to define/explain key terms.*

Candidate A

(c) (ii) To become new species, the two populations must become increasingly different. They won't be able to breed.

Candidate B

(c) (ii) The two populations must not interbreed, so that they become different species.

e Neither candidate fully appreciates the process of speciation: both are awarded just 1 mark. An examiner would be looking for these ideas:
- The populations must be reproductively isolated.
- This would lead to the gene pools becoming increasingly different.
- Interbreeding would eventually be impossible.

e **Both candidates should have been able to score better on this question. They lost marks throughout by not supplying enough detail. Candidate A scores 5 marks and Candidate B scores 6 marks.**

Populations and succession

The diagrams show a primary succession originating in a pond. The graph shows the accompanying changes in biomass, primary production and species diversity.

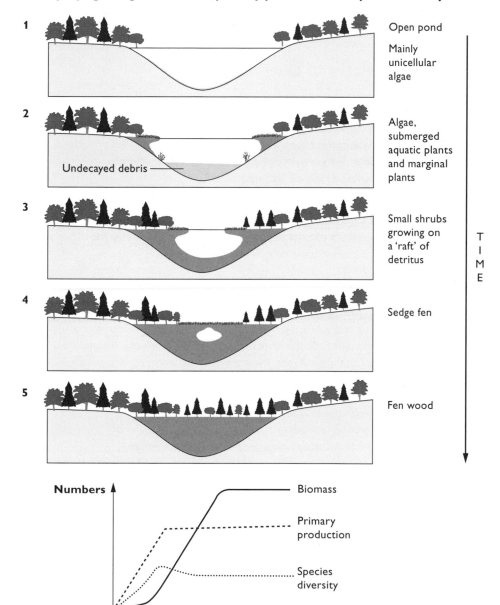

1. Open pond

   Mainly unicellular algae

2. Algae, submerged aquatic plants and marginal plants

   Undecayed debris

3. Small shrubs growing on a 'raft' of detritus

4. Sedge fen

5. Fen wood

TIME

Numbers

Biomass

Primary production

Species diversity

(pioneer)   (climax)   Time

(a) Use the graph and your knowledge of succession to explain the changes occurring in the first three stages. (5 marks)

(b) How could you collect the data needed to calculate the species diversity at stage 4? (5 marks)

Total: 10 marks

■ ■ ■

Candidates' answers to Question 9

Candidate A

(a) As time goes by, more and more different plants start to appear in the pond. Eventually these die and decay and add to the nutrients in the pond. This means that even more plants can survive. Eventually the pond gets filled in with the dead remains of the plants and a fen wood grows on top of it.

Candidate B

(a) The original algae die and decay and add nitrates to the pond water. This allows more and different species of plants to colonise the pond. Some of the dead remains of plants float on the water and provide a new habitat for other plants and small shrubs that start to appear.

Neither candidate has given a good account using all the information in the diagram and the graphs. There is no reference in either answer to the concept of pioneer species (the unicellular algae), although both have the idea of the environment being altered (by increasing ion concentration and the formation of a raft). Neither mentions species diversity, although both talk about an increase in species richness. Candidate A has given a superficial account of succession and has not confined the response to the first three stages, as instructed. Candidate B's response also lacks detail. Both candidates score 2 marks. An examiner would be looking for five of the following ideas:

- The algae are pioneer species.
- As they die and decay, more ions are released into the water.
- Decay is not total and a covering of debris forms on the bottom of the pond.
- The population of algae increases as the primary productivity increases.
- The changed environment allows other species to enter.
- The species diversity index increases so the other species must be successful.
- The productivity continues to rise, so the community is increasing.
- The accumulation of debris forms a raft on which land plants can grow.

Candidate A

(b) You would need to throw some quadrats at random and count the number of organisms of each type in the quadrat. If you got an average, you can calculate the number of each in the area and use this to calculate the species diversity.

Candidate B

(b) To calculate the species diversity, you need to calculate a species diversity index. The formula for this index is:

$$d = (N(N - 1))/(\Sigma n(n - 1))$$

You need to know how many there are of each species in the area. You can actually count the number of big trees, but for small plants and animals, you need to estimate the size of the population. You can use the mark–release–recapture technique to estimate the size of animal populations and random quadrats to estimate the size of plant populations. Use a random number generator and place the quadrats at the coordinates it generates. Count the number of individual plants in each quadrat and scale up to the whole area. You can then use the formula to calculate the diversity index.

Candidate A shows some understanding of sampling using random quadrats, but doesn't really know how the species diversity will be calculated. Candidate A scores 3 marks. Candidate B has given a much fuller answer and would probably score 5 marks. However, some points of detail are missing. You could mention:
- how to estimate the size of the area itself
- how to scale up to the whole area
- some detail of the mark–release–recapture technique

Overall, Candidate A scores 5 marks; Candidate B scores 7.

Photosynthesis and energy transfer

(a) The flow chart summarises the fate of light energy striking a leaf.

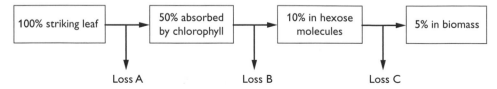

(i)   Give two processes that could contribute to loss **A**.   (2 marks)

(ii) What does loss **B** tell you about the efficiency of the process of photosynthesis? Explain your answer.   (2 marks)

(iii) In this example, what percentage of light energy becomes part of the net primary production? Explain your answer.   (3 marks)

(b) The diagram below summarises the main reactions of the light-independent stage of photosynthesis. The graph shows changes in the levels of RuBP and GP in a chloroplast when the light source is removed.

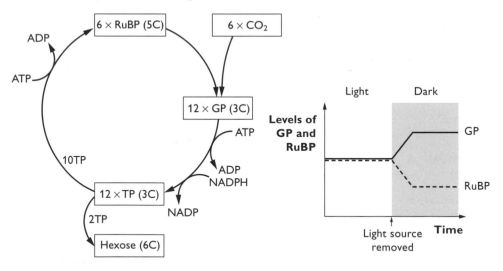

(i)   Give *two* possible fates of the hexose produced.   (2 marks)

(ii) Use the diagram to explain the changes in the levels of RuBP and TP in the chloroplast when the light source is removed.   (6 marks)

Total: 15 marks

Candidates' answers to Question 10

Candidate A

(a) (i) Some of the light misses the leaf and some is reflected back into space.

Candidate B

(a) (i) Of the 50% not absorbed by the chlorophyll, some will be reflected back into space from the leaf surface and some will be the wrong wavelength and so will not be absorbed by the chlorophyll. This may pass through the leaf or be reflected from the chloroplast.

Candidate A has again been careless, and scores only 1 mark. He or she has clearly just seen 'light energy' and 'energy losses' and has produced a stock answer. However, both the stem of the question and the diagram clearly refer to 'light energy *striking the leaf*', and so the first half of the answer is totally inappropriate. Candidate B is awarded 2 marks, and actually has all three of the possible processes. *Read the question carefully and make sure that you don't just respond to a key word or phrase.*

Candidate A

(a) (ii) It shows that it is quite an inefficient process, because there is a considerable loss of energy. Not all the energy absorbed by chlorophyll ends up in hexoses.

Candidate B

(a) (ii) The efficiency of photosynthesis is only 20% (10%/50%) as energy is lost during the chemical reactions.

Both answers are justified from the phrasing of the question. The question does not require that you work out the percentage efficiency — but where the calculation is so straightforward, it is often a good idea. Candidate A, however, doesn't really explain why the efficiency is low, and scores only 1 mark. Candidate B says *where* and *how* the energy is lost and so is awarded both marks.

Candidate A

(a) (iii) 10% because 10% ends up in the hexose molecules.

Candidate B

(a) (iii) 5%. The net primary production is the actual biomass of the organism, not just the sugars formed in photosynthesis.

Candidate A does not understand the concept of net primary production, which is the amount of biomass produced (in a given time) after respiratory losses (loss C in the diagram). Candidate B understands that the permanent biomass reflects the net primary production, but does not explain the idea of respiratory losses (loss C), and so loses 1 of the 3 marks.

Candidate A

(b) (i) It can be stored as glucose or starch.

Candidate B

(b) (i) It can be stored as glucose or converted to cellulose for making cell walls. It can also be converted to amino acids to make proteins or to fatty acids to make lipids. Finally it can be respired to release energy to make ATP.

Candidate A does not really appreciate that hexose is a sugar with six carbon atoms — like glucose. Nor does the candidate appreciate that sugars aren't storage products as they are soluble. However, it could be stored as starch, so 1 mark is awarded. Candidate B has deliberately given not just two fates but five. In this case, all the ones given are correct and so the candidate scores the 2 marks. However, it would be quite easy to produce a list of five in which two or three were wrong. *The examiner will not choose a correct response for you from a list that also includes wrong answers.*

Candidate A

(b) (ii) When the light source is removed, RuBP decreases and GP increases. This is because RuBP is converted to GP in the light-independent reactions. When all the RuBP has been used up, no more GP can be made.

Candidate B

(b) (ii) In the dark reactions, RuBP is converted into GP, which is then converted to TP. Some of this is re-converted back into RuBP. This needs ATP and reduced NADP from the light reactions. When the light is removed, the ATP and reduced NADP cannot be made. Therefore, the RuBP cannot be formed again, so the level falls.

Neither candidate gives a convincing answer. Candidate A *describes* the changes with little explanation; just 2 marks are awarded. Candidate B understands more, but is awarded only 3 of the 6 marks available. An examiner would be looking for the following ideas:

- Both ATP and reduced NADP are produced in the light-dependent stage.
- They are both needed to convert GP to TP.
- ATP is needed to convert TP to RuBP.
- When the light source is removed, these reactions cannot proceed.
- Neither ATP nor reduced NADP is needed to convert RuBP into GP.
- This reaction can still proceed in the dark.
- So the level of GP rises and the level of RuBP falls.

Any six of these ideas would gain full marks.

This is not a difficult question. If you take care in reading it, then most of the sections are quite straightforward. Part (b)(ii) requires application of understanding and examiners would expect a grade-A candidate to score better here. The other sections should be accessible to a grade-C candidate who has prepared thoroughly. Candidate A scores only 5 marks while Candidate B scores 11.